# 50 GREAT STATES
## MINI-BOOKS

BY SYLVIA CHARLESWORTH

SCHOLASTIC
PROFESSIONAL BOOKS

NEW YORK · TORONTO · LONDON · AUCKLAND · SYDNEY
MEXICO CITY · NEW DELHI · HONG KONG · BUENOS AIRES

## DEDICATION

*To Maddie, Dash & Theo*

*Thanks to Rebecca Callan for being such a meticulous and nurturing editor,
and to Jaime Lucero for coming up with a splendid design*

Cover design by Maria Lilja
Interior design by Grafica, Inc.
Interior art by Robin Bernard, Holly Jones, Mona Mark, Teresa Southwell,
George Ulrich, Patricia Wynne, and Dover Publications, Inc.

ISBN 0-439-38464-8

# TABLE OF CONTENTS

I've been traveling these United States for more years than I am willing to admit. The best and most informative times I've had were family road trips combined with camping. The younger kids got the "bed," and I got a tent, or sometimes a hammock strung up between trees. When my children were young, we had an old school bus bought at an auction (for $257). It came with hissing air brakes and a folding door. We did our own renovations by tearing out all the seats, except the one behind the driver. Then we built bunks, a kitchen and table (which converted into a bed), a bathroom of sorts, and loads of storage. What a job!

After we sold Billie, our bus, we moved up to a van and small trailer. With four kids, aged two to fifteen, we hit the road. Although there were occasional outbursts from one or another of us, the biggest trip of over 3,500 miles was a huge success and had a lasting impact on us all. With the exception of Hawaii, we've camped it all (in some states several times). Retirement has made us softies, and we now own a 20-foot recreational vehicle, which is heaven. No more cooking out, standing in knee-high mud holding an umbrella over a sputtering gas stove.

I am more enthusiastic than ever about traveling these magnificent United States and sharing what I've learned. It's my hope that this book will be a classroom resource you can turn to again and again as you celebrate and explore this wonderful country of ours with students.

**—Sylvia Charlesworth**

# INTRODUCTION

## WELCOME TO 50 GREAT STATES MINI-BOOKS!

ake a trip to each state with this collection of 50 illustrated nonfiction mini-books, all packed with interesting, fun-to-read information. Each reproducible mini-book comes complete with an outline map, a look at state history, and fascinating facts about geography, people, and places. Plus, you'll find fun-to-solve word games that reinforce what children have learned and include ways to assess comprehension. The mini-books are an engaging way to teach important social studies content while celebrating all 50 states.

Other features of the *50 Great States Mini-Books* include:

☆ write-on pages that can be personalized by students, helping children demonstrate what they've learned

☆ easy-to-assemble mini-books that students can complete as a class, in groups, or as independent work or homework

☆ handy mini-reference books children can use all year

## Using the Mini-Books in Your Classroom

### Complementing Curriculum

This collection of fact-packed, pocket-sized mini-books gives students a concise summary of the history and geographical features of each state. Designed for maximum flexibility, you can use the mini-books however they best fit your teaching needs. Use them to complement a comprehensive study of the United States, find the specific state your class is currently studying, or use a mini-book that relates to a theme or unit. For example, the Oklahoma mini-book would be a valuable addition to a unit on Westward Expansion. The Arizona mini-book would work well in a study of desert regions or the Grand Canyon.

### Weaving Mini-Books Into the Schedule

The 50 mini-books in this book are arranged alphabetically, but you may use the mini-books in any order and in any combination you wish. For example, if your class is studying Colonial Life, you can use the mini-books for the 13 original colonies. If your class is studying geography, you can order the mini-books according to region, with the Continental Divide as a marker. If you plan to cover all 50 states over the course of the school year, you can tackle a few mini-books each week.

When you're ready to begin teaching with a mini-book, consider the following teaching sequence:

☆ Ask students to discuss what they know about the state. Perhaps some children have traveled in that state or read a story that took place there. Treasure troves of valuable information, children know a lot about geography, museums, landmarks, and so on.

☆ Invite students to assemble and color their mini-books. Read each state mini-book as a shared reading activity. Or, if you prefer, invite students to read them on their own, with a partner, or in small groups. Because they are self-contained, mini-books also work well as homework.

☆ Encourage students to take home the mini-books to share with family members. Before long, your students' home libraries will include a whole collection of mini reference books they can use in their studies—all year!

# Looking Inside the Mini-Book

All 50 mini-books follow the same format, so children can complete each mini-book the same way.

Page 1

**Page 1** is the cover, consisting of an outline map of that particular state indicating the capital; bordering states, countries, or bodies of water; and some noteworthy cities and geographical features.

Pages 2 and 3

**Pages 2 and 3** contain two pages of text about the state, accompanied by a fun-to-solve riddle. Children crack the riddle by placing the underlined letters in order on the blanks.

Page 4

**Page 4** has Fast Facts, including population, size, and other interesting state-specific information.

Page 5

**Page 5** consists of text related to the state, which may be a short biography, geographical feature, historic happening, city profile, sporting event, or more.

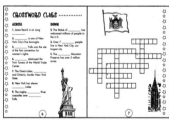

Pages 6 and 7

**Pages 6 and 7** relate to the crossword. Page 6 has lists of clues (drawn from the mini-book text). Page 7 has the crossword puzzle.

Page 8

**Page 8** features the state flag and spaces for students to present two facts they've learned or two thoughts they have about the state. This page also includes the answers for the riddle and crossword.

perforation
here

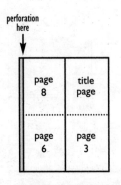

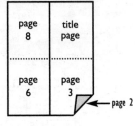

← page 2

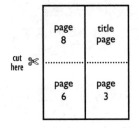

cut
here ✂

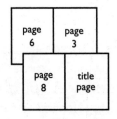

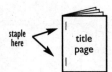

staple
here

# Assembling the Mini-Books

Carefully remove the mini-book to be copied, tearing along the perforation.

Make a double-sided copy of the mini-book for each student. If your machine does not have a double-sided function, make copies of the title page first. (You might want to make extra copies.) Place these copies in the machine's paper tray. Then make a test copy of the second page to be sure that it copies onto the back of the first page. It is important that page 2 copies directly behind the title page.

Once you have a double-sided copy, cut the page in half along the dotted line.

Place page 3 behind the title page, then page 5 behind page 3 and so forth.

Fold the pages in half along the solid line.

Check to be sure that the pages are in proper order, then staple them together along the book's spine.

This book features 50 mini-books that you can use to strengthen knowledge and concepts within every domain of your curriculum. The following are activities you can use to teach with any of the mini-books and extend learning.

**Travel Bureau Posters**  Select the state (or states) you'd like the class to study. Divide the class into small groups. Tell students that each group works for a state travel bureau and has been asked to develop a travel poster that encourages people to visit the state. Ask each group to read and complete the mini-book that corresponds to their state. Then, using the mini-book for reference, have each group design a travel poster.

If your classroom has Internet access, you may want to invite students to visit www.tourstates.com/. It is the official Web site of the National Council of State Tourism Directors and has fast, easy access to the travel bureaus for all 50 states. Just click on a state and your students are linked with tourism information— everything from the state's annual festivals to famous landmarks.

Explain that each poster will need to include a hand-drawn outline map and descriptive writing about interesting places to visit. Ask each group to mark 5–10 travel destinations and the state capital with colorful markers or stickers. When the posters are complete, mount them on a wall or bulletin board. Refer to them as you teach, and your students' learning will be reinforced and their creative efforts supported.

**Trading-Places Stories**  Encourage students to use their newfound knowledge about different states and their imaginations to write narratives. Begin by having students pick a state they might want to visit for a summer, move to, or travel to for a long weekend. Ask children to write a story describing what their experiences would be like in that new state. Ask them

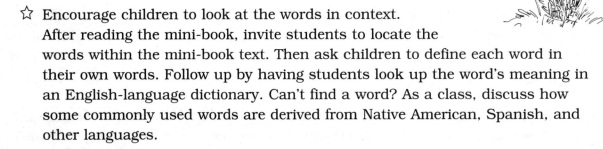

to describe ways in which the state is similar or different from their home state with questions like: *How does the weather compare? What do you notice about the number of cattle compared to people? The amount of wetlands compared to desert? The prevalence of farms compared to industrial areas?* and so on.

Take this activity a step further by having students create bar graphs that spotlight specific similarities and differences between the states. For example, if a child chose to compare Maine with Arizona he or she might make a graph comparing the temperature highs and lows.

**All-Star Vocabulary Words**   The 100 words listed on page 11 are drawn from the text of the mini-books, with two words from each state. Here are some suggestions for using them:

☆  Review the vocabulary words before reading the mini-book, so students won't stumble over unfamiliar words.

☆  Encourage children to look at the words in context. After reading the mini-book, invite students to locate the words within the mini-book text. Then ask children to define each word in their own words. Follow up by having students look up the word's meaning in an English-language dictionary. Can't find a word? As a class, discuss how some commonly used words are derived from Native American, Spanish, and other languages.

☆  Ask students to alphabetize some or all of the words listed. You may want to work with groups of words instead of the whole list. For example, if your class is studying the New England states, have students place just those six states in alphabetical order (Connecticut, Maine, Massachusetts, New Hampshire, Rhode Island, and Vermont).

**These key vocabulary words are listed in order from Alabama to Wyoming to reflect the way the mini-books have been alphabetically ordered in this book.**

| | | | | | |
|---|---|---|---|---|---|
| **Alabama** | simulator | antebellum | **Montana** | smokejumper | icons |
| **Alaska** | permafrost | Iditarod | **Nebraska** | mammoth | prospectors |
| **Arizona** | saguaro | Gila | **Nevada** | extraterrestrial | hemisphere |
| **Arkansas** | spelunkers | Confederacy | **New Hampshire** | planetarium | velocity |
| **California** | eureka | sequoia | **New Jersey** | delectable | Victorian |
| **Colorado** | centennial | continental | **New Mexico** | enchantment | UFO |
| **Connecticut** | beluga | scrimshaw | **New York** | suffragettes | immigration |
| **Delaware** | ratified | Constitution | **North Carolina** | shoals | feat |
| **Florida** | peninsula | manatee | **North Dakota** | albino | scoria |
| **Georgia** | endured | inducted | **Ohio** | skywalk | assassinated |
| **Hawaii** | luau | lava | **Oklahoma** | sooner | homesteaders |
| **Idaho** | raptors | encampment | **Oregon** | migration | caldera |
| **Illinois** | manufacture | skyscraper | **Pennsylvania** | Amish | unanimous |
| **Indiana** | Hoosier | significant | **Rhode Island** | solitary | amendments |
| **Iowa** | maize | bloomers | **South Carolina** | palmetto | Gullah |
| **Kansas** | solo | enforced | **South Dakota** | Badlands | conservationist |
| **Kentucky** | currency | thoroughbred | **Tennessee** | depression | volunteer |
| **Louisiana** | bayou | Cajun | **Texas** | armadillo | rallying |
| **Maine** | contiguous | skirmish | **Utah** | monument | hoodoo |
| **Maryland** | indented | migrating | **Vermont** | producer | quarry |
| **Massachusetts** | debates | marathon | **Virginia** | Pentagon | confiscated |
| **Michigan** | abolitionist | revolutionized | **Washington** | spawn | avalanche |
| **Minnesota** | terminus | folklore | **West Virginia** | secede | mosaic |
| **Mississippi** | syndicated | sensational | **Wisconsin** | serpent | badger |
| **Missouri** | Ragtime | apprenticed | **Wyoming** | fumaroles | geyser |

☆ **Charlesworth, Sylvia.** *50 Great States Read & Solve Crossword Puzzles.* Scholastic Professional Books, 2002.

☆ **Different Authors.** *America the Beautiful Series.* Children's Press, 2000.

☆ **English, June A. & Jones, Thomas D.** *Encyclopedia of the U.S. at War.* Scholastic Inc., 1999.

☆ **Fielding's Travel Guide Staff.** *Fielding's Freewheelin' USA.* Fielding Worldwide, Inc., 1999.

☆ **King, Daniel.** *First Facts About U.S. History.* Gale Group, 1996.

☆ **Leedy, Loreen.** *Celebrate the 50 States.* Holiday House Inc., 1999.

☆ *Merriam-Webster's Collegiate Encyclopedia: The Ultimate Desk Reference.* Merriam-Webster, Inc., 2000.

☆ **Miller, Millie, et al.** *The United States of America: A State-by-State Guide.* Scholastic Inc., 1999.

☆ *Road Atlas midsize 2002—United States, Canada and Mexico.* Rand-McNally, 2001.

☆ **Rubel, David.** *The United States in the 20th Century.* Scholastic Inc., 1995.

☆ **Wright, John.** *Sticker Atlas of the United States and Canada.* Troll Communications L.L.C., 1998.

☆ **Written by Kids.** *The Kids' Book of the 50 Great States.* Scholastic Professional Books, 1998.

☆ **Zeman, Anne & Kelly, Kate.** *Everything You Need to Know About American History Homework: A Desk Reference for Students & Parents.* Scholastic Inc., 1994.

**Here are two more facts I found, or two thoughts I have, about the great state of ALABAMA:**

1. _____

_____

2. _____

_____

Answer to Riddle: Monarch butterfly
Answers to Crossword: Across: 1. Helen 5. Montgomery 7. Civil 8. Florida 9. Rosa;
Down: 1. Huntsville 2. Birmingham 3. Camellia 4. Boycott 6. War

---

# ALABAMA
## THE HEART OF DIXIE

TENNESSEE

Huntsville
Tennessee River

Appalachian Mountains

Birmingham

MISSISSIPPI

GEORGIA

Montgomery

Alabama River

FLORIDA

Mobile

GULF OF MEXICO

WELCOME TO THE 22nd State!

**Name:** _____

---

# CROSSWORD CLUES ··············

## ACROSS

**1.** A childhood illness left _____ Keller deaf and blind.

**5.** The capital of Alabama is _____.

**7.** "Ante-bellum" means before the _____ War.

**8.** The state of _____ is south of Alabama.

**9.** _____ Parks refused to give her bus seat to a white man.

## DOWN

**1.** The U.S. Space and Rocket Center is in _____, Alabama.

**2.** _____ is home to the Civil Rights Institute.

**3.** The state flower of Alabama is the _____.

**4.** To _____ means to stop using or buying something as a protest.

**6.** The *USS Alabama* fought in World _____ II.

---

the Battleship Memorial Park, you can check out two "heroes" of World War II: the *USS Alabama* and the submarine *USS Drum.* Birmingham has a Civil Rights Institute that pays tribute to Dr. Martin Luther King, Jr., and others who fought for equal rights. Sports greats are honored at Alabama's Sports Hall of Fame. The state has something for everyone!

*Solve this riddle by placing the underlined letters in order on the blanks.*

# RIDDLE ·················

I am the state insect of Alabama, but I migrate to Mexico in the winter. I have orange wings with a black border and black veins and spots. I taste terrible. I am a

_ _ _ _ _ _ _   _ _ _ _ _ _ _ _

# WELCOME TO ALABAMA

The rocket that took the first men to the moon was developed at the Space and Rocket Center in Huntsville. At the center, you can see what it feels like to be an astronaut by becoming weightless in a zero-gravity machine or by guiding a spacecraft over Mars in a simulator. Then you can tour an antebellum (before the Civil War) mansion built more than 150 years ago. Enjoy the beaches on the Gulf of Mexico in Mobile, the state's only seaport. At

2

7

## ALABAMA FAST FACTS ·············

**Population:** 4,447,100 (23rd largest)
**Size:** 50,744 square miles (29th largest)
**Year Admitted to the Union:** 1819 (22nd state admitted)
**State Flower:** Camellia
**State Dance:** Square dance
**State Nut:** Pecan
**State Bird:** Yellowhammer
**State Saltwater Fish:** Fighting tarpon

**The State Drama of Alabama is *The Miracle Worker* by William Gibson.**

This is the inspiring story of teacher Anne Sullivan and her student Helen Keller, who was blind and deaf.

4

# ROSA PARKS

Rosa Parks was born in Tuskegee, Alabama. As an adult, she worked as a seamstress in the capital city of Montgomery. One day in 1955 Rosa was very tired, but she was ordered to give her bus seat to a white man. She refused and was arrested. Dr. Martin Luther King, Jr., and other civil rights activists urged a boycott of the bus system to protest segregation. People had to walk many miles to and from work every day, but they did it. Their dedication to fair treatment for all helped the Civil Rights Movement gain recognition. The Civil Rights Institute in Birmingham tells their story.

5

**Here are two more facts I found, or two thoughts I have, about the great state of ALASKA:**

1. _____

   _____

2. _____

   _____

Answer to Riddle: Glacier
Answers to Crossword: Across: 1. Gold 5. Mendenhall 7. Bigger 8. Juneau 9. Russia;
Down: 2. Denali 3. Iditarod 4. Flag 6. Sun 7. Bering

---

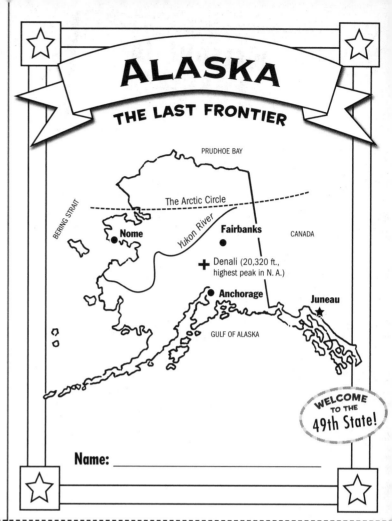

# ALASKA
## THE LAST FRONTIER

PRUDHOE BAY

The Arctic Circle

BERING STRAIT

Nome

Yukon River

Fairbanks

CANADA

+ Denali (20,320 ft., highest peak in N. A.)

Anchorage

Juneau

GULF OF ALASKA

WELCOME TO THE 49th State!

Name: _____

---

# CROSSWORD CLUES

### ACROSS

**1.** The Klondikers came looking for _____.

**5.** The _____ Glacier is near Juneau.

**7.** No state in the United States is _____ than Alaska.

**8.** The capital of Alaska is _____.

**9.** The United States bought Alaska from _____.

### DOWN

**2.** _____ is the tallest mountain in North America.

**3.** The yearly dog sled race from Anchorage to Nome is the _____.

**4.** Alaska's _____ has the Big Dipper and the North Star.

**6.** Alaska is sometimes called the "Land of the Midnight _____."

**7.** To the west of Alaska is the _____ Strait.

---

reached by float planes or boats. One exception to this is the Alaskan Highway (1,523 miles), which is built on permanently frozen soil (permafrost). Alaska's cities offer spectacular sights. Juneau is framed by the Mendenhall Glacier. Skagway was built for the Klondike Gold Rush. Alaska's motto, "North to the future," says a lot about our 49th state.

Solve this riddle by placing the underlined letters in order on the blanks.

# RIDDLE

I am big, blue, and made from compacted snow. A bay in Alaska is named after me.

I am a _ _ _ _ _ _ _ .

## WELCOME TO ALASKA

In 1867, the U.S. purchased Alaska from Russia for the bargain price of two cents an acre. We bought a magnificent collection of riches: oil, gold, timber, abundant wildlife, and excitement. "The Last Frontier" is one-fifth as big as all our other states combined. Alaska is cold; part of it is above the Arctic Circle, where the sun doesn't rise in winter and doesn't set in summer (Land of the Midnight Sun). Because roads are generally scarce, much of Alaska can only be

## ALASKA FAST FACTS ·················

**Population:** 626,932 (48th largest)

**Size:** 571,951 square miles (largest)

**Year Admitted to the Union:** 1959 (49th state admitted)

**State Sport:** Dog mushing

**State Festival:** Ice Climbing Festival (Valdez, February)

**State Mineral:** Gold

**State Fish:** King salmon

**State Tree:** Sitka spruce

**State Motto:** North to the future

> **Alaska has more private planes *per capita* (per person) than any other state!**
>
> In remote areas, pilots may find only a landing strip and no airport.

## THE IDITAROD RACE

The first Iditarod Race was held on March 3, 1973, to commemorate an event from 1925. In that year, children in the city of Nome were dying from a diphtheria outbreak, and 20 mushers (dog sled drivers) rushed in serum to save them. The Iditarod Race covers about 1,152 miles from Anchorage to Nome. Depending on the weather, the drivers' skill, and the determination of the dogs, the race can take up to 17 days. Sleds are made from wood (ash), with leather lashings and steel- or aluminum-covered runners. The dogs eat 5,000 calories a day and wear booties on their paws. Winners receive a cash prize and the honor of having run a great race!

**Here are two more facts I found, or two thoughts I have, about the great state of ARIZONA:**

1. _____
   _____

2. _____
   _____

Answer to Riddle: Geronimo
Answers to Crossword: Across: 5. Desert 7. Phoenix 8. Ride 9. Cactus 10. Colorado;
Down: 1. Wren 2. Nevada 3. Mexico 4. Frogs 6. Tribal

(8)

---

# ARIZONA
## THE GRAND CANYON STATE

UTAH

COLORADO

NEVADA

Colorado River

Grand Canyon

The Four Corners

● Flagstaff

NEW MEXICO

Colorado River

● Lake Havasu City

CALIFORNIA

Phoenix ★

● Yuma

The Sonoran Desert

● Tombstone

WELCOME TO THE 48th State!

MEXICO

**Name:** _____

---

# CROSSWORD CLUES • • • • • • • • • • • •

### ACROSS

**5.** Much of Arizona is _____.

**7.** The capital of Arizona is _____.

**8.** You can _____ a mule to the bottom of the Grand Canyon and back.

**9.** The saguaro is a _____.

**10.** The _____ River carved out the Grand Canyon.

### DOWN

**1.** Arizona's state bird is the cactus _____.

**2.** Only the state of _____ is growing faster than Arizona.

**3.** The country south of Arizona is _____.

**4.** In Arizona, there are _____ that live in trees.

**6.** The Hopi have _____ lands in Arizona.

(6)

---

monsters (poisonous lizards), rattlesnakes, and other exotic animals live in Arizona. Phoenix, Tucson, Flagstaff, and Scottsdale are important cities. But in Lake Havasu City, you can see the London Bridge, which really was brought over from England! It's not hard to see why Arizona is the second fastest growing state (after Nevada)!

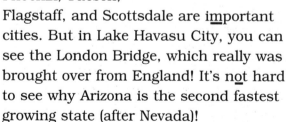

Solve this riddle by placing the underlined letters in order on the blanks.

# RIDDLE • • • • • • • • • • • • • • • • • •

I was a famous Apache chief from Arizona who fought long and hard for my people.

My name is _ _ _ _ _ _ _ _ .

(3)

# WELCOME TO ARIZONA

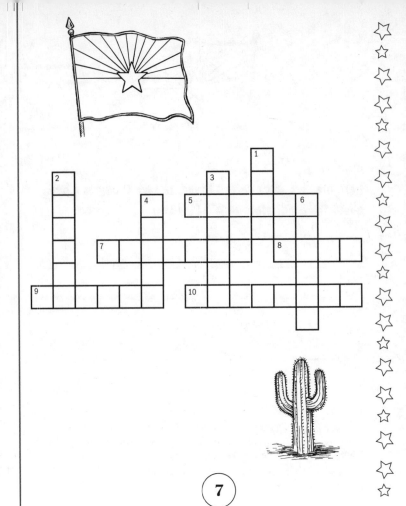

**A**rizona is two-thirds desert, which makes the state sunny, dry, and beautiful. Full of memorable places such as the Petrified Forest and the Grand Canyon, its scenery is often featured in movies. The state contains 40 percent of Native American tribal lands and is home to Hopis, Apaches, Navajos, and other tribes. Saguaro National Park and Organ Pipe National Monument protect cactuses, some of which are 30 feet tall and over 200 years old. Gila

## ARIZONA FAST FACTS

**Population:** 5,130,632 *(20th largest)*

**Size:** 113,635 square miles *(6th largest)*

**Year Admitted to the Union:** 1912 *(48th state admitted)*

**State Bird:** Cactus wren

**Sunniest City in the U.S.:** Yuma

**State Flower:** Saguaro cactus blossom

**State Neckwear:** Bola tie

**Oldest Continually Occupied City in America:** Oraibi

> **The state amphibian is the Arizona Tree Frog.**
>
> It lives in forests 5,000 feet above sea level.

# THE GRAND CANYON

**A**rizona boasts one of the seven natural wonders of the world: the Grand Canyon. Over thousands of years, the Colorado River has cut the canyon out of rock. The Grand Canyon is 277 miles long, a mile deep, and 18 miles across at its widest point. Snow closes the canyon's North Rim most of the year, but the South Rim is usually open for the millions of people who visit each year. Tourists can ride the Grand Canyon Railway from Williams, Arizona. Hardy folks hike or ride mules to the floor of the canyon and back, or raft down the Colorado River's rapids.

Here are two more facts I found, or two thoughts I have, about the great state of ARKANSAS:

1. _____
   _____

2. _____
   _____

---

# ARKANSAS
## THE NATURAL STATE

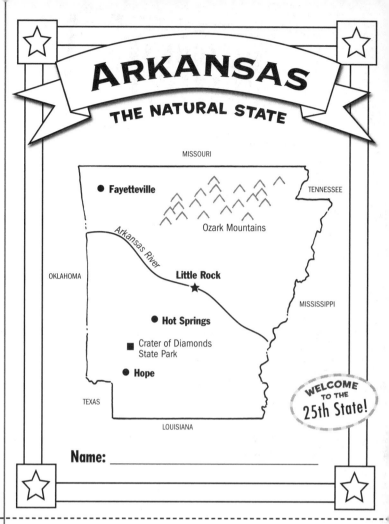

MISSOURI

● Fayetteville

Ozark Mountains

Arkansas River

OKLAHOMA

Little Rock ★

TENNESSEE

● Hot Springs

■ Crater of Diamonds State Park

MISSISSIPPI

● Hope

TEXAS

LOUISIANA

WELCOME TO THE 25th State!

Name: _____

---

# CROSSWORD CLUES

## ACROSS

**3.** You'll feel at home in Arkansas if you play the _____.

**5.** Arkansas is the _____ State.

**7.** The capital of Arkansas is _____ _____.

**8.** Arkansas joined the Confederacy during the _____ War.

**9.** The water at _____ Springs is warm and pure.

**10.** Our national bird is the bald _____.

## DOWN

**1.** Tennessee and _____ are the states east of Arkansas.

**2.** Sam _____ was the founder of Wal-Mart.

**4.** The letter *F* in 143 degrees F is the abbreviation for _____.

**6.** Our 42nd President was William Jefferson _____.

---

Confederacy during the Civil War. Today the state appeals to new industries, workers, and retirees. Our 42nd President, William Jefferson Clinton, was born in Hope. He was elected Governor of Arkansas at the age of 32. Sam Walton, founder of the biggest corporation in the United States, opened the first Wal-Mart in Rogers, Arkansas, in 1962.

Solve this riddle by placing the underlined letters in order on the blanks.

# RIDDLE

I am the hardest, naturally occurring substance in the world, am very valuable, and can be found for free in a state park in Arkansas.

I am a _ _ _ _ _ _ _ .

# WELCOME TO ARKANSAS

**A**rkansas is nicknamed the Natural State because it has exceptional natural gifts such as forests, streams, hot springs, and mountains. The state welcomes hikers, spelunkers (cave explorers), prospectors, and folks who like to fish. The Ozark and Ouachita Mountains are home to the Ozark Folk Festival and the National Fiddle Championships. The flatter part of the state snuggles up to the Mississippi River and is good for farming. Arkansas joined the

---

---

# ARKANSAS FAST FACTS ·············

**Population:** 2,673,400 (33rd largest)

**Size:** 52,068 square miles (27th largest)

**Year Admitted to the Union:** 1836 (25th state admitted)

**State Drink:** Milk

**First Woman Elected to the U.S. Senate:** Hattie Caraway

**Winter Home of:** Bald eagle (our national bird)

**State Musical Instrument:** Fiddle

**State Bird:** Mockingbird

**The honeybee is the state insect.**

It keeps very busy making honey.

---

# HOT SPRINGS AND HOT SPRINGS NATIONAL PARK

**I**magine a drop of rain falling on an Arkansas mountaintop 4,000 years ago. It slowly made its way 4,000 to 8,000 feet underground, where Earth's temperature is 143 degrees F. There it warmed naturally in a stone catch basin. Thousands of years later, through cracks in the Earth's surface, it bubbled up in Hot Springs, Arkansas. Millions of gallons of this pure water—which is the ideal temperature for a relaxing (some say healing) bath—were piped into bathhouses. Visitors still bathe in the hot springs and drink the water bubbling from city fountains in the hope that it will improve their health.

**CALIFORNIA REPUBLIC**

**Here are two more facts I found, or two thoughts I have, about the great state of CALIFORNIA:**

1. _____

   _____

2. _____

   _____

Answer to Riddle: Redwood
Answers to Crossword: Across: 3. Sacramento 6. Golden 7. Monterey 8. Francisco
9. Mendocino; Down: 1. Bear 2. Population 3. Sequoias 4. Coast 5. Reagan

(8)

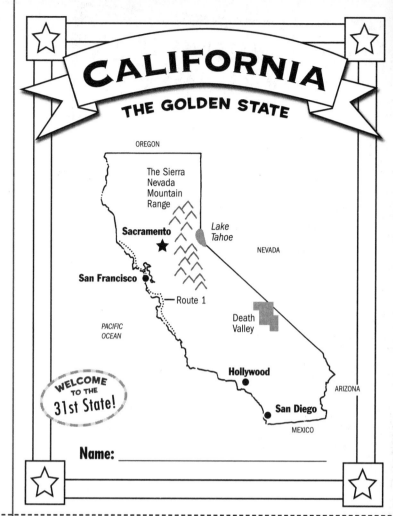

# CALIFORNIA
## THE GOLDEN STATE

OREGON

The Sierra
Nevada
Mountain
Range

Sacramento ★

Lake Tahoe

NEVADA

San Francisco ●

Route 1

PACIFIC OCEAN

Death Valley

Hollywood ●

ARIZONA

San Diego ●

MEXICO

WELCOME TO THE 31st State!

Name: _____

---

# CROSSWORD CLUES ·············

### ACROSS

**3.** The capital of California is _____.

**6.** California is the _____ State.

**7.** There is an aquarium on _____ Bay.

**8.** The Golden Gate Bridge is in San _____.

**9.** Art and architecture can be enjoyed in _____.

### DOWN

**1.** The flag of California has a _____ on it.

**2.** California has the largest _____ of all the United States.

**3.** _____ and redwoods are related.

**4.** Route 1 runs along the _____ of California.

**5.** Ronald _____ was the 40th President of the United States.

(6)

---

HOLLYWOOD

could enjoy breathtaking scenery in Yosemite National Park and ride a cable car, or savor the Death Valley heat and take in the beauty of Lake Tahoe. Or you could visit Father Junipero Serra's 21 missions on *El Camino Real* (the Royal Road). The freshest fruits and vegetables grow in California. New and creative ideas thrive in the Golden State, too!

Solve this riddle by placing the underlined letters in order on the blanks.

# RIDDLE ·············

I am over 350 feet tall, 20 feet across, 1,500 years old, and am a member of the sequoia family. I live on the fog-shrouded coast of northern California.

I am a _ _ _ _ _ _ _ .

(3)

# WELCOME TO CALIFORNIA

California is first in population and th<u>ir</u>d in size. The state's motto is "Eur<u>e</u>ka," which means, "I have found it"—and many people *have* found what they were seeking in the Golden State. The "49ers" sought go<u>l</u>d. Actors found fame in Holly<u>wo</u>od. Ronald Reagan, our 40th President, was a movie star. Silicon Valley is the heart of the c<u>o</u>mputer industry. In one very busy day, you could ski in the Sierras and then surf in the Pacific Ocean. You

# CALIFORNIA FAST FACTS ·············

**Population:** 33,871,648 (largest)

**Size:** 158,693 square miles (3rd largest)

**Year Admitted to the Union:** 1850 (31st state admitted)

**Endangered Species:** California condor

**State Fossil:** Saber-toothed cat

**Baseball Teams:** Angels, Dodgers, Athletics, Padres, Giants

**First McDonald's:** San Bernardino (in 1948)

**Theme Park:** Disneyland (opened in 1955 in Anaheim)

> **Death Valley recorded the highest U.S. temperature.**
>
> In 1913, the temperature reached 134 degrees F.

# CALIFORNIA ROUTE 1—THE PACIFIC COAST HIGHWAY

Traveling along Route 1, which follows most of California's Pacific coastline, is a spectacular adventure. The scenery, including pounding ocean surf and jagged cliffs marking the edge of the highway, is unmatched anywhere in the world. You can view sea otters and sea lions in their natural habitats or take a break from the highway and tour the Hearst Castle in San Simeon. Enjoy the Big Sur area—Carmel and Pebble Beach—but be sure to visit the aquarium on Monterey Bay. San Francisco has the Golden Gate Bridge, and Mendocino offers fine art and architecture.

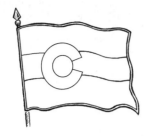

**Here are two more facts I found, or two thoughts I have, about the great state of COLORADO:**

1. _____
   _____

2. _____
   _____

Answer to Riddle: Molly Brown
Answers to Crossword: Across: 4. Mint 6. Acclimate 8. Denver 9. Durango 10. Mile;
Down: 1. Centennial 2. Peak 3. Skiing 5. America 7. Colorado

---

# COLORADO
## THE CENTENNIAL STATE

WYOMING    NEBRASKA

NEBRASKA

● Fort Collins

**Denver** ★

UTAH

The Rocky
Mountains

**Colorado Springs**
●

KANSAS

✛
Pikes
Peak

The Four
Corners    ● **Durango**

Continental Divide

NEW MEXICO    OKLAHOMA

WELCOME
TO THE
**38th State!**

**Name:** _____

---

# CROSSWORD CLUES ··············

## ACROSS

**4.** The letter "D" on our coins signifies the Denver _____.

**6.** People must _____ themselves to Colorado's high altitude.

**8.** The capital of Colorado is _____.

**9.** You can see bronco-busting at a rodeo in _____.

**10.** A _____ is 5,280 feet.

## DOWN

**1.** A birthday that celebrates 100 years is a _____.

**2.** The slogan on the west-ward wagons read "Pikes _____ or Bust."

**3.** The stripes on Colorado's flag celebrate _____.

**5.** Katherine Lee Bates wrote "_____ the Beautiful."

**7.** _____ means "red rocks."

---

up in the Pacific. The capital, Denver, is nicknamed the Mile High City because it is 5,280 feet above sea level. It has a United States mint that manufactures about 75 percent of our coins and is the second-largest depository of our gold. Durango has rodeos, white-water rafting, and a steam-operated railroad. Skiers flock to Aspen, Vail, and other top resorts.

Solve this riddle by placing the underlined letters in order on the blanks.

# RIDDLE ··············

I struck it rich in the Colorado silver mines and was nicknamed "Unsinkable" because I survived the Titanic disaster.

I am __ __ __ __ __  __ __ __ __ __ .

## WELCOME TO COLORADO

**C**olorado means "red rocks" in Spanish. It is the Centennial State because it joined the Union on our 100th birthday (1876). The state's Rocky Mountains have 55 peaks over 14,000 feet high and a national park to honor them. The air is thin at these altitudes, so people have to acclimate (gradually get used to it). The ridge of the Rockies forms the Continental Divide. Rain falling east of this divide eventually flows to the Atlantic Ocean. Rain falling to the west winds

(2)

(7)

## COLORADO FAST FACTS

**Population:** 4,301,261 (24th largest)

**Size:** 103,718 square miles (8th largest)

**Year Admitted to the Union:** 1876 (38th state admitted)

**State Flag:** Two blue for skis; one white stripe for snow

**State Flower:** Columbine

**Famous Astronaut:** Scott Carpenter (orbited Earth in Mercury)

**State Fossil:** Stegasaurus

**The Steamboat Springs High School Marching Band is the only band in the world to do this.**

**The band performs on skis.**

(4)

## PIKES PEAK OR BUST

**P**ikes Peak is named after Zebulon Montgomery Pike, who tried unsuccessfully to climb it. The peak is so tall that it is visible from the Great Plains. In 1858, gold was discovered in Colorado. Over 100,000 people headed west. They traveled in wagons bearing the slogan "Pikes Peak or Bust." Some panned for gold in the rivers. Some dug with picks and shovels or used dynamite. In 1893, the view from the peak's summit inspired Katherine Lee Bates to write "America the Beautiful." Today Pikes Peak is only one of the jewels in Colorado's crown.

(5)

Here are two more facts I found, or two thoughts I have, about the great state of CONNECTICUT:

1. _____

_____

2. _____

_____

8

---

# CONNECTICUT
## THE CONSTITUTION STATE

MASSACHUSETTS

The Canaan Mountains

● Litchfield

★ Hartford

NEW YORK

Connecticut River

Thames River

RHODE ISLAND

Groton ●
● Mystic

New Haven ●

LONG ISLAND SOUND

WELCOME TO THE 5th State!

Name: _____

---

# CROSSWORD CLUES

## ACROSS

**2.** The name of the first nuclear-powered submarine is the _____.

**5.** Connecticut's first laws were a model for the U.S. _____.

**7.** The state song of Connecticut is "Yankee _____ Dandy."

**8.** _____ Aquarium is home to beluga whales and penguins.

**9.** Delicately carved designs on whales' teeth are called _____.

## DOWN

**1.** Connecticut's capital is _____.

**3.** _____ is the biggest industry in Connecticut.

**4.** Many _____ lived and worked in Connecticut.

**5.** The U.S. _____ Guard Academy is in New London, Connecticut.

**6.** Only _____ states are smaller than Connecticut.

6

---

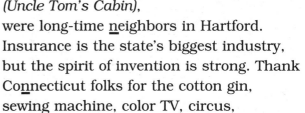

Mark Twain (*Tom Sawyer*) and Harriet Beecher Stowe (*Uncle Tom's Cabin*), were long-time <u>n</u>eighbors in Hartford. Insurance is the state's biggest industry, but the spirit of invention is strong. Thank Co<u>n</u>necticut folks for the cotton gin, sewing machine, color TV, circus, helicopter, Frisbee, and lollipop!

Solve this riddle by placing the underlined letters in order on the blanks.

# RIDDLE

My mascot is a husky dog. I am the University of Connecticut, but most people call me

_ _ _ _ _ .

3

# WELCOME TO CONNECTICUT

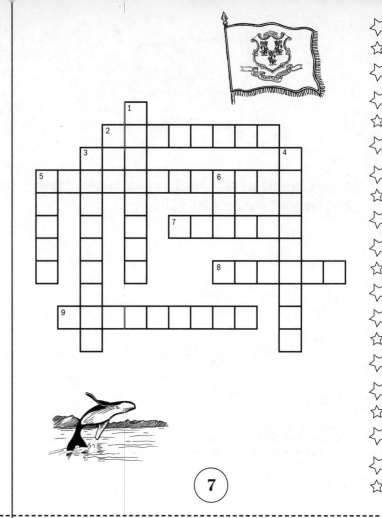

**C**onnecticut is known as the Constitution State because its first laws were a model for our U̲.S. Constitution. The state's easy access to the Atlantic Ocean has given it a proud seafaring history. The U.S. C̲oast Guard Academy is in New London. The first nuclear-powered submarine, the *Nautilus,* can be toured in Groton. Noah Webster compiled his famous dictionary in Connecticut, and our oldest newspaper, the *Hartford Courant,* began there, too. Tw̲o famous writers,

## CONNECTICUT FAST FACTS ···········

**Population:** 3,405,565 (29th largest)

**Size:** 4,845 square miles (48th largest)

**Year Admitted to the Union:** 1788 (5th state admitted)

**State Insect:** Praying mantis

**State Song:** "Yankee Doodle Dandy"

**Famous University:** Yale University

**Famous Collection of Dinosaur Fossils:** Peabody Museum

**Woman Governor:** Ella Grasso (elected in 1974)

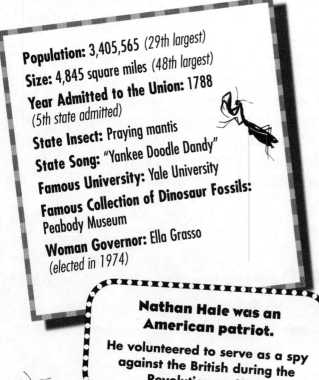

> **Nathan Hale was an American patriot.**
>
> He volunteered to serve as a spy against the British during the Revolutionary War.

# MYSTIC

**V**isiting Mystic is like going back to the mid-1800s, when the fastest clipper ships and the first regular ironclad vessel were built there. Today the Mystic Aquarium houses 3,500 living sea creatures, including beluga whales and black-footed penguins. On display at the seaport is the last wooden whaling ship, plus models of other ships and figureheads. Whales were hunted for food and oil for lamps. Fishermen created scrimshaw by carving intricate designs on whales' teeth or bones. Now many whale species are near extinction. Whale-watching trips offer excitement without harming the animals.

Here are two more facts I found, or two thoughts I have, about the great state of DELAWARE:

1. _____

_____

2. _____

_____

Answer to Riddle: Ladybug
Answers to Crossword: Across: 2. DuPont 5. Wilmington 7. Ratify 8. Smaller 9. Dover
10. Hudson; Down: 1. Chickens 3. Pentagon 4. Lewes 6. Beach

8

# DELAWARE
## THE FIRST STATE

PENNSYLVANIA

Newark ● ● Wilmington

*Chesapeake and Delaware Canal*

★ Dover    *St. Jones River*

*DELAWARE BAY*

MARYLAND

● Lewes

*Rehoboth Bay*

MARYLAND

WELCOME TO THE 1st State!

Name: _____

---

# CROSSWORD CLUES ·············

## ACROSS

**2.** The _____ Company produces chemicals.

**5.** The first log cabin built in America was near _____.

**7.** To _____ is to approve in an official manner.

**8.** Only one state, Rhode Island, is _____ than Delaware.

**9.** The capital of Delaware is _____.

**10.** Henry _____ was a famous navigator and explorer.

## DOWN

**1.** Soldiers during the Revolutionary War often carried blue hen _____.

**3.** A five-sided shape is called a _____.

**4.** Ferries cross the Delaware Bay from _____, Delaware.

**6.** Vacationers flock to Rehoboth _____.

6

---

with them. Today, thanks to the du Pont family, Delaware is noted for its chemical industry and inventions (nylon, Teflon, Mylar), plus major developments in the automotive and electronics fields. Reho<u>b</u>oth Beach is a pop<u>u</u>lar resort town on the Atlantic Ocean. Farther north, ferries chu<u>g</u> across Delaware Bay from Lewes, Delaware, to Cape May, New Jersey.

# RIDDLE ·············

Solve this riddle by placing the underlined letters in order on the blanks.

The school children of Delaware conducted a write-in campaign to have me named the state insect.

I am a _ _ _ _ _ _ _ .

3

# WELCOME TO
# DELAWARE

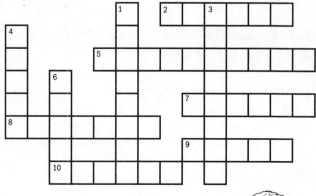

**D**elaware is called the First State because it was the first state to ratify (approve officially) our Constitution. John Dickinson, called the "Penman of the American Revolution," wrote the Articles of Confederation protesting British rule. Colonists gathered on the "Green" in Dover with their muskets to join General George Washington in the fight for independence. Volunteer soldiers wore blue uniforms and often carried blue hen chickens

# DELAWARE FAST FACTS ···············

**Population:** 783,600 (45th largest)

**Size:** 1,954 square miles (49th largest)

**Year Admitted to the Union:** 1787
(1st state admitted)

**Named After:** Lord de la Warr, first Governor of the Virginia Colony

**First Log Cabin in America:** Wilmington

**Famous Astronomer:** Annie Jump Cannon
(1863–1941)

**State Motto:** Liberty and Independence

**State Drink:** Milk

**Fort Delaware is located on Pea Patch Island.**

**The five-sided fort was built in the shape of a pentagon.**

# INDEPENDENCE

**I**n 1609, the Lenni-Lenape Indians (called the Delaware by the British) were probably the first people to spot Captain Henry Hudson as he sailed the *Half Moon* into Delaware Bay. The first European settlers in Delaware were the Dutch, followed by the Swedes, and then by the English. The state was given to William Penn as part of Pennsylvania (Penn's woods), but in 1704 Penn allowed Delaware to have its own legislature. Delaware cast the deciding vote for independence at the Continental Congress in Philadelphia. The state fought for the Union during the Civil War.

Here are two more facts I found, or two thoughts I have, about the great state of FLORIDA:

1. _____

_____

2. _____

_____

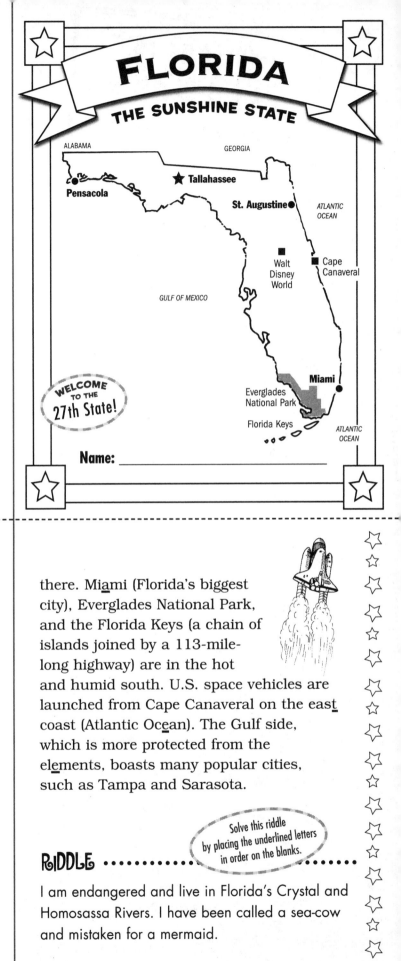

# FLORIDA
## THE SUNSHINE STATE

ALABAMA — GEORGIA
★ Tallahassee
Pensacola ●
St. Augustine ●
ATLANTIC OCEAN
■ Walt Disney World
■ Cape Canaveral
GULF OF MEXICO
WELCOME TO THE 27th State!
Miami ●
Everglades National Park
Florida Keys
ATLANTIC OCEAN

Name: _____

---

# CROSSWORD CLUES ··············

## ACROSS

**2.** The city of St. Augustine was founded by _____.

**4.** The _____ Space Center is at Cape Canaveral.

**5.** The biggest cruise port and the biggest city in Florida is _____.

**7.** _____ is the capital of Florida.

**9.** Walt Disney World is near _____.

**10.** _____ teams train in Florida.

## DOWN

**1.** _____ National Park has alligators, crocodiles, snakes, and mosquitoes!

**3.** _____ are reptiles in the crocodile family.

**6.** At the tip of Florida are several islands called the Florida _____.

**8.** Florida's _____ is about 4,000 miles long.

---

there. Miami (Florida's biggest city), Everglades National Park, and the Florida Keys (a chain of islands joined by a 113-mile-long highway) are in the hot and humid south. U.S. space vehicles are launched from Cape Canaveral on the east coast (Atlantic Ocean). The Gulf side, which is more protected from the elements, boasts many popular cities, such as Tampa and Sarasota.

# RIDDLE ··············

Solve this riddle by placing the underlined letters in order on the blanks.

I am endangered and live in Florida's Crystal and Homosassa Rivers. I have been called a sea-cow and mistaken for a mermaid.

I am a _ _ _ _ _ _ _ .

# WELCOME TO FLORIDA

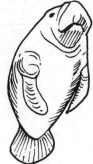

**A** large stretch of land projecting into water is a peninsula. The peninsula of Florida extends into the Atlantic Ocean and the Gulf of Mexico. The state has 4,000 <u>mi</u>les of coastline.

More species of fish are found in Florida's waters than anywhere else in the world. The north has a temperate climate. St. Augustine (founded by Spaniards in 1565), Tallahassee (the capital), and Pensacola (on the panhandle) are located

---

# FLORIDA FAST FACTS ·················

**Population:** 15,982,378 *(4th largest)*
**Size:** 53,927 square miles *(22nd largest)*
**Year Admitted to the Union:** 1845
*(27th state admitted)*
**State Shell:** Horse conch
**First Baseball Training Camp:** Jacksonville *(1888)*
**Major Crops:** Citrus fruits
**Largest Cruise Ship Port:** Miami

**The Daytona 500 used to be run on Daytona Beach.**

**The current speedway is a 2.5 mile tri-oval track.**

---

# VACATIONLAND

**F** lorida, the Sunshine State, is perfect for vacationers. The most popular destination is the Walt Disney World Resort near Orlando. It offers four theme parks, three water parks, five golf courses, a campground, and a dozen hotels. Universal Studios has rides and entertainment based on popular movies and TV shows, and Seaworld features marine life. The Kennedy Space Center offers tours and exhibits for space buffs. Busch Gardens offers thrill rides, Sanibel has shells, Sarasota showcases the circus, and the Everglades have alligators. Florida is full of sun, surf, sand, and fun!

Here are two more facts I found, or two thoughts I have, about the great state of GEORGIA:

1. _____

_____

2. _____

_____

---

# GEORGIA
## THE PEACH STATE

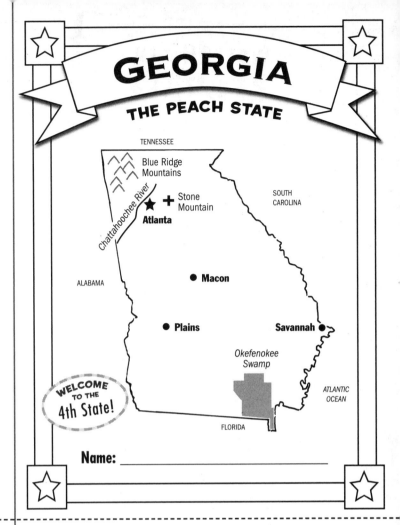

TENNESSEE

Blue Ridge Mountains

SOUTH CAROLINA

Chattahoochee River

+ Stone Mountain

★ **Atlanta**

ALABAMA

● **Macon**

● **Plains**

**Savannah** ●

*Okefenokee Swamp*

ATLANTIC OCEAN

FLORIDA

WELCOME TO THE 4th State!

**Name:** _____

---

# CROSSWORD CLUES ··············

## ACROSS

**1.** Jackie Robinson was a famous _____ player.

**3.** _____ Woods is the youngest winner of the Masters Tournament.

**5.** The 1996 Summer _____ were held in Atlanta.

**7.** Peaches and _____ are important crops in Georgia.

**8.** _____ was founded as a settlement for debtors.

**9.** Dr. Martin Luther _____, Jr., was born in Atlanta in 1929.

## DOWN

**2.** The capital of Georgia is _____.

**3.** General Oglethorpe founded Georgia as the _____ (and last) colony.

**4.** Georgia is named after King George II of _____.

**6.** Off the coast of Georgia are the very popular Golden _____.

---

Ridge Mountains (part of the Appalachians), a beautiful coastline with the famous Golden Isles offshore, orchards filled with peaches, bumper crops of peanuts, and famous sons and daughters. The civil rights leader Dr. Martin Luther King, Jr., was born in Atlanta. Our 39th President, Jimmy Carter, hailed from Plains. Juliette Low, founder of Girl Scouts of the USA, was also from Georgia.

# RIDDLE ·················

Solve this riddle by placing the underlined letters in order on the blanks.

Some people call me a goober. I am a versatile and nutritious legume grown plentifully in Georgia.

I am a _ _ _ _ _ _ .

# WELCOME TO GEORGIA

**G**eorgia was first inhabited by the Creek and Cherokee Indians. In 1733, it was founded as the 13th and last colony by General James Oglethorpe. He began an English settlement at Savannah as a refuge for debtors (people who owed money). Atlanta, the capital city, was burned to the ground during our Civil War. It has rebounded as a center of transportation, commerce, and sports. In 1996, the city hosted the Summer Olympics. Georgia has mountains, the Blue

---

# GEORGIA FAST FACTS

**Population:** 8,186,453 (10th largest)

**Size:** 57,906 square miles (21st largest)

**Year Admitted to the Union:** 1788 (4th state admitted)

**State Flower:** Cherokee rose

**Largest State East of the Mississippi River:** Georgia

**Named After:** King George II of England

**Youngest Winner of Masters Golf Tournament in Augusta:** Tiger Woods

**Soft Drink Begun in Atlanta Drug Store:** Coca-Cola

**State Song:** "Georgia on My Mind"

**Stone Mountain is the largest exposed mass of granite in the world.**

It's decorated with carvings of Jefferson Davis, Robert E. Lee, and Stonewall Jackson.

---

# JACKIE ROBINSON

**J**ackie Robinson was a champion on and off the field. Born in Cairo, Georgia, he was the first African American to play baseball in the major leagues. An outstanding athlete, he had to leave college to help his mother raise the family. After serving as a second lieutenant during World War II, Robinson played for the Kansas City Monarchs in the Negro Leagues. Branch Rickey spotted his talents and signed him with the Brooklyn Dodgers. Robinson endured taunts but was named Rookie of the Year in 1947. With a career batting average of .311, he was inducted into the Baseball Hall of Fame.

Here are two more facts I found, or two thoughts I have, about the great state of HAWAII:

1. _____

_____

2. _____

_____

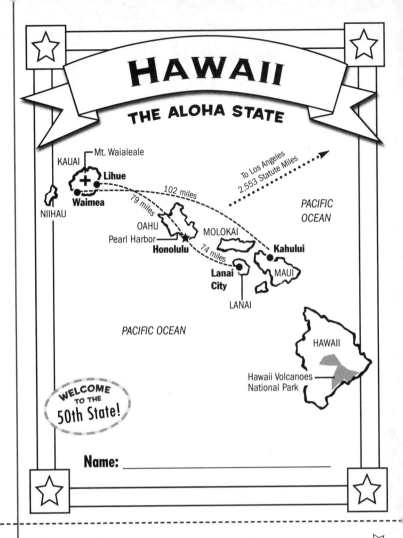

# HAWAII
## THE ALOHA STATE

KAUAI — Mt. Waialeale
Lihue
Waimea
NIIHAU
OAHU
Pearl Harbor
Honolulu
MOLOKAI
Lanai City
LANAI
MAUI
Kahului
To Los Angeles 2,553 Statute Miles
102 miles
79 miles
74 miles
PACIFIC OCEAN
PACIFIC OCEAN
HAWAII
Hawaii Volcanoes National Park

WELCOME TO THE 50th State!

Name: _____

# CROSSWORD CLUES · · · · · · · · · · · ·

**ACROSS**

**1.** _____ is the goddess of fire.

**6.** The capital of Hawaii is _____.

**7.** The Humuhumunukunukuapua is the state _____ of Hawaii.

**8.** _____ is one of the official languages of Hawaii.

**9.** The U.S. entered World War II when Pearl _____ was bombed.

**10.** There are over _____ different cultures and races in Hawaii.

**DOWN**

**2.** The state of Hawaii has _____ principal islands.

**3.** Hawaii was formed (and is still being formed ) by _____.

**4.** Liliuokalani was the last _____ of Hawaii.

**5.** Hawaii, admitted to the United States in 1959, is our _____ state.

Humuhumunukunukuapua. The word *aloha* means "hello," "good-bye," "welcome," "good luck," and "love." Hawaii is noted for beautiful vacation spots featuring sun, surf, scenery, and luaus (elaborate feasts). Telescopes atop Mauna Kea make Hawaii an astronomy center. In 1941, Japan bombed Pearl Harbor, which triggered our entry into World War II.

*Solve this riddle by placing the underlined letters in order on the blanks.*

# RIDDLE · · · · · · · · · · · · · · · · · · · · ·

I am the principal crop of Hawaii. Some people even love me on pizza!

I am _ _ _ _ _ _ _ _ _ .

# WELCOME TO HAWAII

Hawaii is located in the central Pacific Ocean. It consists of eight principal islands and more than 100 islets formed by undersea volcanic activity. First settled by Polynesians from the Marquesas Islands, Hawaii now has the world's most diverse population, with 60 different races and cultures. The two official languages are English and the very musical Hawaiian, which contains only 12 letters (including all five vowels). The state fish is the

## HAWAII FAST FACTS • • • • • • • • • • • • • • •

**Population:** 1,211,537 (42nd largest)

**Size:** 6,423 square miles (47th largest)

**Year Admitted to the Union:** 1959 (50th state admitted)

**Most Populated Hawaiian Island:** Oahu

**Famous for the Sport of:** Surfing

**Wettest Spot on Earth:** Mount Waialeale (460 inches of rain annually)

**Birth Announced by a Comet:** Kamehameha the Great (1758–1819)

**State Flower:** Yellow hibiscus

**Queen Liliuokalani (1838–1917) was the last Hawaiian ruler.**

She was also the last queen to live in the only palace in the United States.

## VOLCANOES

Volcanoes are vents in Earth's crust that allow steam and lava to surface. A build-up of pressure causes an eruption that fills the earth and sky with fire, extreme heat, and flowing red-hot lava. It can take a century for lava to cool. Hawaii Volcanoes National Park is home to the volcano Mauna Loa, which is snow-capped in winter. Hawaiian legend says that Pele, the goddess of fire, resides in the volcano Kilauea. Volcanic activity continually changes Hawaii by creating new land, increasing the area of the island chain by an average of four inches every year.

Here are two more facts I found, or two thoughts I have, about the great state of IDAHO:

**1.** _____

_____

**2.** _____

_____

Answer to Riddle: Hells Canyon
Answers to Crossword: Across: 2. Sun 4. Deer 6. Potatoes 7. Boise 8. Hells
9. Canada; Down: 1. Raptors 2. Shoshone 3. Lewis 5. River

---

# IDAHO
## THE GEM STATE

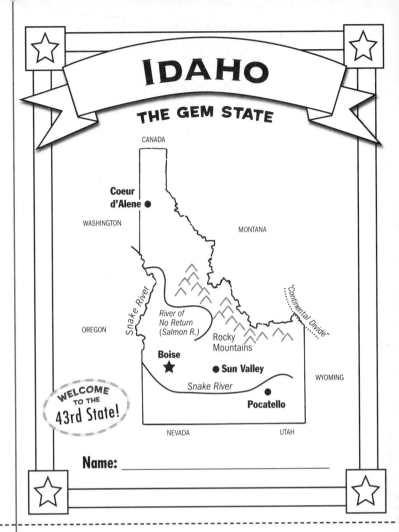

**WELCOME TO THE 43rd State!**

**Name:** _____

---

# CROSSWORD CLUES ·············

## ACROSS

**2.** _____ Valley is a famous ski resort.

**4.** Caribou are in the _____ family.

**6.** _____ are the main crop of Idaho.

**7.** The capital of Idaho is _____.

**8.** _____ Canyon is the deepest gorge in North America.

**9.** The country of _____ is on Idaho's 45-mile-wide northern border.

## DOWN

**1.** _____ are celebrated at the World Center for Birds of Prey in Boise.

**2.** Sacagawea was a _____ Indian.

**3.** The _____ and Clark Expedition successfully traveled to the Pacific.

**5.** Another name for the Salmon _____ is "The _____ of No Return."

---

45 miles wide at its northern border with Canada and 310 miles across in the south. The south, irrigated by the Snake River, is where they grow those fine Idaho potatoes. The city of Lewiston is connected to the Pacific Ocean by the Columbia River. NASA astronauts trained on the lava fields of Craters of the Moon National Monument.

*Solve this riddle by placing the underlined letters in order on the blanks.*

# RIDDLE ·············

I form part of the Idaho-Oregon boundary and reach a depth of 7,900 feet. This makes me the deepest gorge in North America.

I am _ _ _ _ _   _ _ _ _ _ _

# WELCOME TO
# IDAHO

A cre for acre, Idaho has more wilderness than any other state. It has deep canyons, rushing rivers, towering mountains, spectacular lakes, and dense forests. This wilderness entices skiers, hikers, white-water rafters, and all kinds of nature lovers. Raptors (birds of prey) such as eagles, falcons, and hawks, dominate the skies. Caribou, moose, cougars, beaver, mink, and otters roam the rivers and forests. Trout, salmon, and bass swim in the rivers. Idaho is

(2)

(7)

## IDAHO FAST FACTS

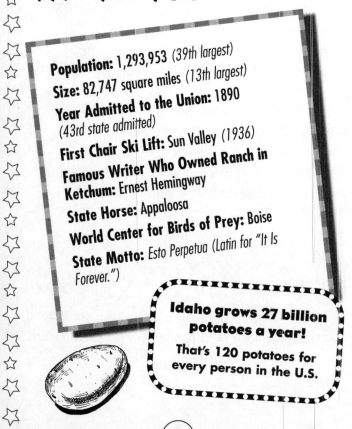

**Population:** 1,293,953 (39th largest)

**Size:** 82,747 square miles (13th largest)

**Year Admitted to the Union:** 1890 (43rd state admitted)

**First Chair Ski Lift:** Sun Valley (1936)

**Famous Writer Who Owned Ranch in Ketchum:** Ernest Hemingway

**State Horse:** Appaloosa

**World Center for Birds of Prey:** Boise

**State Motto:** Esto Perpetua (Latin for "It Is Forever.")

### Idaho grows 27 billion potatoes a year!
That's 120 potatoes for every person in the U.S.

(4)

# LEWIS & CLARK EXPEDITION

I n 1803, Thomas Jefferson bought the Louisiana Territory from France for 15 million dollars. This amazing bargain, known as the Louisiana Purchase, included territory stretching from the Mississippi to the Rockies and from the Gulf of Mexico to Canada. President Jefferson engaged Meriwether Lewis and William Clark to lead and chart an overland expedition across this area to the Pacific Ocean. Forty men with various skills traveled up the Missouri River to what is now North Dakota and built Fort Mandan to serve as winter encampment. Sacagawea, a Shoshone Indian, joined the group at the fort. She obtained horses, interpreted, and helped guide the explorers to success.

(5)

Here are two more facts I found, or two thoughts I have, about the great state of ILLINOIS:

1. _____

_____

2. _____

_____

Answer to Riddle: Ferris wheel
Answers to Crossword: Across: 3. Prairie 6. Skyscraper 8. Springfield 9. Chicago
10. Lincoln; Down: 1. Mississippi 2. Transportation 4. El 5. Windy 7. Michigan

---

# ILLINOIS
## THE PRAIRIE STATE

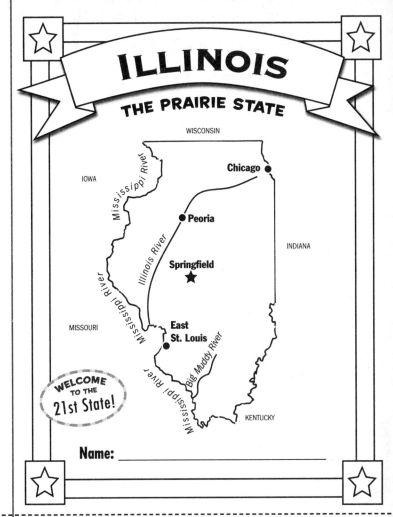

WISCONSIN

IOWA

Mississippi River

Chicago

Illinois River

Peoria

INDIANA

Springfield ★

Mississippi River

MISSOURI

East
St. Louis

Big Muddy River

Mississippi River

KENTUCKY

WELCOME
TO THE
21st State!

Name: _____

---

# CROSSWORD CLUES

## ACROSS

**3.** The _____ State has flat land and fertile soil made by glaciers.

**6.** The Sears Tower in Chicago is a _____.

**8.** The capital of Illinois is _____.

**9.** The 3rd largest city in the United States is _____.

**10.** The Land of _____ is named for President Abraham _____.

## DOWN

**1.** The _____ River is on the western border of Illinois.

**2.** Illinois is a major _____ center.

**4.** "_____" is short for elevated train.

**5.** Chicago is nicknamed the _____ City.

**7.** Superior, _____, Huron, Erie, and Ontario are the Great Lakes.

---

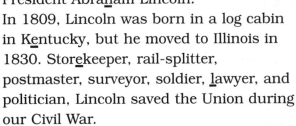

busiest rail and air centers in the world, including Chicago's O'Hare Airport. Illinois—the Land of Lincoln—is proud of President Abraham Lincoln. In 1809, Lincoln was born in a log cabin in Kentucky, but he moved to Illinois in 1830. Storekeeper, rail-splitter, postmaster, surveyor, soldier, lawyer, and politician, Lincoln saved the Union during our Civil War.

Solve this riddle by placing the underlined letters in order on the blanks.

# RIDDLE

I was born in Illinois. I'm tall, have seats, go around and around, and live in amusement parks and fairs.

I am a _____ _____.

# WELCOME TO ILLINOIS

Years ago, glaciers rolled across what is now Illinois and flattened the land into fertile prairie. Using this soil to their advantage, Illinois farmers raise corn, wheat, soybeans, dairy products, hogs, and cattle. The state is also a leader in the manufacture of farm equipment. Situated on Lake Michigan, one of the Great Lakes, Illinois has access to the Atlantic Ocean and to the Gulf of Mexico by way of the Mississippi. As a major transportation center, it also boasts the

---

# ILLINOIS FAST FACTS

**Population:** 12,419,293 (5th largest)

**Size:** 55,584 square miles (24th largest)

**Year Admitted to the Union:** 1818 (21st state admitted)

**Famous Entertainer:** Walt Disney (born in Illinois in 1901)

**North America's Tallest Building:** Sears Tower

**State Bird:** Cardinal

**State Flower:** Violet

**Home of the Chicago Cubs:** Wrigley Field

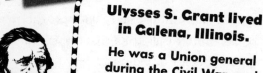

**Ulysses S. Grant lived in Galena, Illinois.**

He was a Union general during the Civil War, and became our 18th President.

# CHICAGO

The first skyscrapers rose in Chicago, our third largest city. Folklore says that in 1871 Mrs. O'Leary's cow kicked over a lantern, starting a fire that destroyed much of the city. But Chicago came back better than ever. Nicknamed the Windy City—perhaps because its politicians talked so much—the city is a center for commerce, transportation, education, and art. Architect Frank Lloyd Wright lived and built masterpieces in nearby Oak Park. Every few seconds an airplane takes off or lands at O'Hare Airport, while the El (elevated train) circles the Loop around downtown.

**Here are two more facts I found, or two thoughts I have, about the great state of INDIANA:**

1. _____

   _____

2. _____

   _____

Answer to Riddle: Bat
Answers to Crossword: Across: 1. Museum 5. Bats 6. Basketball 8. Indy 9. Dunes
10. Hoosier; Down: 2. Santa 3. Caves 4. Band 7. Amish

---

Lake Michigan

MICHIGAN

● South Bend

● Gary

Wabash River

ILLINOIS

★ Indianapolis

OHIO

Wabash River

Wyandotte Caves ■

● Santa Claus

KENTUCKY

WELCOME TO THE 19th State!

**Name:** _____

---

# CROSSWORD CLUES ··············

## ACROSS

**1.** The largest children's _____ in the world is in Indianapolis.

**5.** _____ are valuable because they eat bugs.

**6.** The sport of _____ is very popular in Indiana.

**8.** The Indianapolis 500 is nicknamed the _____ 500.

**9.** The _____ in Indiana are along Lake Michigan.

**10.** No one knows for sure where the word _____ came from.

## DOWN

**2.** Indiana has a town named _____ Claus.

**3.** The Wyandotte _____ have 35 miles of underground passages.

**4.** If you play in a _____, your instrument was probably made in Indiana.

**7.** There is a large _____ settlement near Shipshewana.

---

and pharmaceuticals. Industrial areas providing oil, steel, and other commodities are centered near Gary, Fort Wayne, and Evansville. Many Hoosiers are big basketball fans, but are proud of their other sports teams, too. The biggest children's museum in the world is in the capital of Indianapolis, which also has excellent sports facilities and clean, safe streets. Go, Hoosiers!

*Solve this riddle by placing the underlined letters in order on the blanks.*

# RIDDLE ···············

Some people are afraid of me, but I provide a valuable service by eating tons of bugs. I am an endangered species in Indiana.

I am a _ _ _ .

# WELCOME TO INDIANA

There are several explanations for Indiana's nickname, the Hoosier State. It might be the question, "Who's here?" Or it might refer to Sam Hoosier, who hired Indiana workers to build a canal in Kentucky. A skilled Amish community near Shipshewana guarantees bountiful farms and flea markets stocked with crafts such as hand-made wooden furniture and quilts. Nearby Elkhart produces 50 percent of all our band instruments— plus recreational vehicles

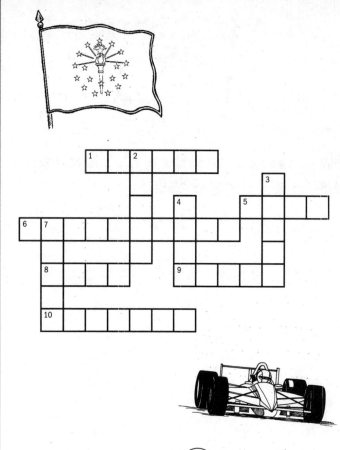

## INDIANA FAST FACTS

**Population:** 6,080,485 (14th largest)
**Size:** 35,867 square miles (38th largest)
**Year Admitted to the Union:** 1816 (19th state admitted)
**State Bird:** Cardinal
**Noted for:** Covered bridges
**Underground Caverns:** Wyandotte Caves (35 miles)
**Indiana Dunes:** Located on Lake Michigan
**State Motto:** Crossroads of America

**The Raggedy Ann doll was created by Marcella Gruelle.**

She produced the doll in Indianapolis in 1914.

# THE INDIANAPOLIS 500

The Indianapolis (Indy) 500 is the largest sporting event in the world. Each May over 400,000 fans attend the auto race, which began in 1911. The race, which lasts for 500 bone-rattling miles, is run on a 2.5-mile asphalt oval at the Indianapolis Motor Speedway. Drivers in formula cars that feature rear engines and open cockpits compete for prizes topping $1.5 million. The raceway started as a testing ground for Indiana's auto industry and has led to significant advances such as balloon tires, rearview mirrors, and improved fuel.

IOWA

**Here are two more facts I found, or two thoughts I have, about the great state of IOWA:**

1. _____

_____

2. _____

_____

Answer to Riddle: Delicious
Answers to Crossword: Across: 2. Maize 6. Grass 7. Livestock 8. Hoover 9. Apples
10. Chief; Down: 1. Hawkeye 3. Baseball 4. Bloomer 5. Goldfinch

# IOWA
## THE HAWKEYE STATE

MINNESOTA

SOUTH DAKOTA

Effigy Mounds ■
(Indian burial mounds)

WISCONSIN

Iowa River

● Sioux City

Cedar Rapids ●

Des Moines ★

■ Loess Hills
(fine wind-blown clay)

Amana Colonies ●

NEBRASKA

ILLINOIS

MISSOURI

WELCOME TO THE 29th State!

Name: _____

---

# CROSSWORD CLUES ··············

## ACROSS

**2.** _____ is another name for corn.

**6.** Corn and _____ are in the same family.

**7.** Farm animals like hogs and cattle are called _____.

**8.** Herbert _____ was the 31st President of the United States.

**9.** Lightning striking a tree led to the development of Delicious _____.

**10.** Black Hawk was an Indian _____.

## DOWN

**1.** Iowa is the _____ State.

**3.** The movie *Field of Dreams* is about _____.

**4.** Bloomers (baggy women's pants) were named for Amelia _____.

**5.** The American _____ is the state bird of Iowa.

---

manufactures kitchen appliances. F.L. Maytag invented the hand-cranked washing machine in Newton. The Writer's Workshop at the University of Iowa educates some of our finest authors. *The Music Man* by Meredith Wilson is based on Mason City, and the Ringling Brothers began their circus in McGregor. Our 31st President, Herbert Hoover, was born and is buried at West Branch.

Solve this riddle by placing the underlined letters in order on the blanks.

# RIDDLE ··············

In the 1800s, lightning struck an apple tree in Iowa. From the shoots farmers developed an apple called

_ _ _ _ _ _ _ _ _

# WELCOME TO
# IOWA

C orn, a member of the grass family, was introduced to settlers by American Indians, who called it maize. Today, the main diet of livestock (pigs and cattle) is corn. Iowa, Illinois, Ohio, Missouri, Kansas, Indiana, and Nebraska make up our corn belt. Their farmers do an excellent job of providing us with food. A religious group from Germany founded the Amana Colonies, which grew into a company that

IOWA

## IOWA FAST FACTS ··················

**Population:** 2,926,324 (30th largest)

**Size:** 55,869 square miles (25th largest)

**Year Admitted to the Union:** 1846 (29th state admitted)

**Famous Field:** Dyersville (where the baseball movie Field of Dreams was filmed)

**Famous Artist:** Grant Wood (American Gothic)

**State Bird:** American goldfinch

**Famous Bandleader:** Glenn Miller

**Movie Star:** John Wayne (born Marion Robert Morrison in Winterset in 1907)

**Amelia Bloomer introduced women to wearing pants called bloomers.**

A suffragette, Bloomer lived in Council Bluffs for 40 years.

# CHIEF BLACK HAWK (1767-1838)

I owa is nicknamed the Hawkeye State after Chief Black Hawk. In 1804, a treaty was drawn up that called for the removal of the Sauk and Fox Indians from Illinois to Iowa. Chief Black Hawk, who fought for the British against the U.S. in the War of 1812, declared the treaty worthless and resisted. In 1831, a new treaty forced the Indians to move. But in 1832, Black Hawk and 400 followers crossed back over the Mississippi River and returned to their land in Illinois. The tragic Black Hawk War began. Although Black Hawk survived the war, most Indians left the area.

## Panel (page 8)

Here are two more facts I found, or two thoughts I have, about the great state of KANSAS:

1. _____

_____

2. _____

_____

Answer to Riddle: Tornado
Answers to Crossword: Across: 3. Abilene 6. Earhart 8. Sunflower 9. Buffalo
10. Topeka; Down: 1. Wheat 2. Jayhawkers 4. Brown 5. Eisenhower 7. Wild

(8)

## Panel (page — Kansas cover)

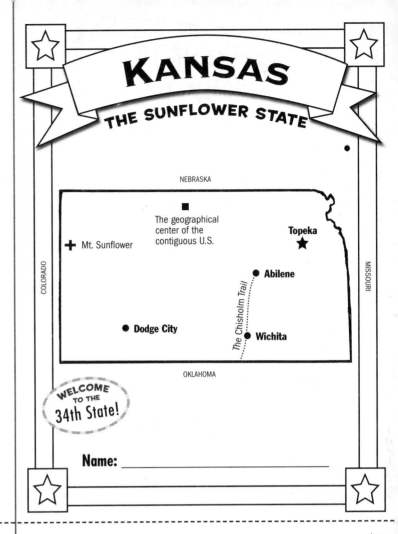

# KANSAS
## THE SUNFLOWER STATE

NEBRASKA

The geographical center of the contiguous U.S.

+ Mt. Sunflower

Topeka ★

COLORADO

● Abilene

The Chisholm Trail

● Dodge City

● Wichita

MISSOURI

OKLAHOMA

WELCOME TO THE
34th State!

Name: _____

## CROSSWORD CLUES ··············

### ACROSS

**3.** The Eisenhower Library is in _____.

**6.** Amelia _____ disappeared when she tried to fly around the world.

**8.** Kansas is the _____ State.

**9.** "_____ Bill" Cody was a hunter and a showman.

**10.** The capital of Kansas is _____.

### DOWN

**1.** Kansas produces more _____ than any other state.

**2.** People from Kansas are nicknamed _____.

**4.** _____ vs. the Topeka Board of Education was a lawsuit before the Supreme Court concerning segregation in public schools.

**5.** Dwight _____ was a famous general and our 34th President.

**7.** Dodge City, Kansas, part of the _____ West, had outlaws and gunfights.

(6)

## Panel (page 3)

Carry Nation (who fought the drinking of alcohol by smashing saloons), the Dalton Gang, Wyatt Earp, and Bat Masterson all wound up in Kansas's Wild West. The state was known as Bleeding Kansas because of the fight over whether it would enter the Union as a free or a slave state. The lawsuit *Brown vs. the Topeka Board of Education* ended segregation in U.S. public schools.

Solve this riddle by placing the underlined letters in order on the blanks.

## RIDDLE ·············

Kansas leads the world in storms like me. I am a highly destructive whirling column of air. I whisked Dorothy and Toto to the Land of Oz.

I am a _ _ _ _ _ _ _ .

(3)

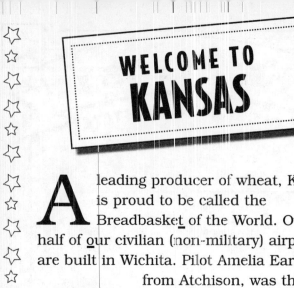

# WELCOME TO KANSAS

**A** leading producer of wheat, Kansas is proud to be called the Breadbasket of the World. Over half of our civilian (non-military) airplanes are built in Wichita. Pilot Amelia Earhart, from Atchison, was the first woman to fly solo across the Atlantic. Pioneer wagons carrying settlers west on the Oregon Trail and cowboys herding cattle up the Chisholm Trail from Texas turned Kansas into a bustling state.

**2**

*(Crossword puzzle with numbered squares 1–10)*

**7**

# KANSAS FAST FACTS

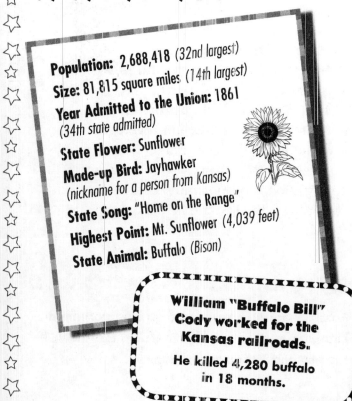

**Population:** 2,688,418 (32nd largest)
**Size:** 81,815 square miles (14th largest)
**Year Admitted to the Union:** 1861 (34th state admitted)
**State Flower:** Sunflower
**Made-up Bird:** Jayhawker (nickname for a person from Kansas)
**State Song:** "Home on the Range"
**Highest Point:** Mt. Sunflower (4,039 feet)
**State Animal:** Buffalo (Bison)

William "Buffalo Bill" Cody worked for the Kansas railroads.

He killed 4,280 buffalo in 18 months.

**4**

# GENERAL DWIGHT D. EISENHOWER

**D**wight David Eisenhower grew up in Kansas. Ike and his wife, Mamie, are buried on the grounds of the Eisenhower Library in Abilene. A graduate of West Point, he was the Supreme Commander of Allied Forces during World War II. Eisenhower made the decision to launch D-Day on June 6, 1944, which led to the eventual defeat of Adolf Hitler. Elected President in 1952, Eisenhower attempted to contain the growth of the communist world. He enforced desegregation by sending federal troops to Little Rock, Arkansas, and he also conceived of our system of interstate highways.

**5**

## Here are two more facts I found, or two thoughts I have, about the great state of KENTUCKY:

1. _____

_____

2. _____

_____

Answer to Riddle: Muhammad Ali
Answers to Crossword: Across: 5. Daniel 7. Bluegrass 8. Mining 9. Frankfort
10. Horses; Down: 1. Davis 2. Fifteenth 3. Derby 4. Boxer 6. Caverns

---

# KENTUCKY
## THE BLUEGRASS STATE

OHIO

INDIANA

Louisville • Frankfort ★

Churchill Downs

WEST VIRGINIA

ILLINOIS

• Fort Knox     • Lexington

MISSOURI

■ Abraham Lincoln Birthplace

Mammoth Cave ■ National Park

Appalachian Mountains

Cumberland Gap

VIRGINIA

TENNESSEE

WELCOME TO THE 15th State!

**Name:** _____

---

# CROSSWORD CLUES ··············

## ACROSS

**5.** _____ Boone blazed the Wilderness Trail.

**7.** Kentucky is the _____ State.

**8.** Coal _____ is a big industry in Kentucky.

**9.** The capital of Kentucky is _____.

**10.** Thoroughbred _____ thrive on Kentucky's calcium-rich grass.

## DOWN

**1.** Jefferson _____ was President of the Confederacy.

**2.** Kentucky was the _____ state admitted to our Union.

**3.** The Kentucky _____ is run at Churchill Downs.

**4.** Many people say Muhammad Ali is the greatest _____ of all time.

**6.** Over 200 animal species inhabit the _____ of Mammoth Cave National Park.

---

the world. Over 200 <u>a</u>nimal species inhabit its 340 miles of un<u>d</u>erground passages. Our country's gold reserve is stored under heavy security at Fort Knox. Confederate President Jefferson Davis and Union President <u>A</u>braham Lincoln were born <u>l</u>ess than 100 miles apart in Kentucky. The state stayed with the Un<u>i</u>on, but many Kentuckians fought for the South.

*Solve this riddle by placing the underlined letters in order on the blanks.*

# RIDDLE ··············

Many people say he was the greatest boxer ever. He said, "I float like a butterfly, sting like a bee." He was born in Louisville, Kentucky, in 1942.

He is \_ \_ \_ \_ \_ \_ \_ \_ \_ \_ \_ .

# WELCOME TO KENTUCKY

Daniel Boone blazed (marked) the Wilderness Trail through the Cumberland Mountains. Following it on foot or horseback, thousands of settlers poured into Kentucky or continued farther west. Tobacco farming and coal mining are major industries in the state as are growing vegetables, fruit, and grass seed; raising horses; and publishing books in Braille. Mammoth Cave National Park is the largest known system of caves in

---

---

# KENTUCKY FAST FACTS

**Population:** 4,041,769 (25th largest)

**Size:** 39,728 square miles (37th largest)

**Year Admitted to the Union:** 1792 (15th state admitted)

**Famous Country Singer:** Loretta Lynn ("Coal Miner's Daughter")

**State Motto:** United We Stand, Divided We Fall

**World's Largest Baseball Bat:** At the Louisville Slugger Museum

**State Flower:** Goldenrod

**Famous Supreme Court Justice:** Louis Brandeis (born in Louisville in 1856)

**Bill Monroe played with the Blue Grass Boys.**

**Monroe is considered to be the father of bluegrass music.**

---

# THE KENTUCKY DERBY

In spring, the grass of Kentucky blooms with blue flowers, so it's easy to see how the Bluegrass State got its name. This calcium-rich grass nourishes the state's thoroughbred horses. High-spirited, slim, and sensitive, these horses are noted for jumping and racing. Since 1875, on the first Saturday in May, the Kentucky Derby has been run at Churchill Downs. The track distance is 1.25 miles, and the Run for the Roses lasts for about two very exciting minutes. Fancy parties and clothes add zest to the celebration. The Kentucky Derby, Preakness Stakes, and Belmont Stakes make up the Triple Crown of U.S. horse racing.

**Here are two more facts I found, or two thoughts I have, about the great state of LOUISIANA:**

1. _____

_____

2. _____

_____

Answer to Riddle: Pelican
Answers to Crossword: Across: 1. Muddy 3. Jefferson 4. Boot 7. Alligators 8. Big;
Down: 1. Marsalis 2. Levees 4. Bayou 5. Mardi 6. Baton

8

---

# LOUISIANA
## THE PELICAN STATE

ARKANSAS

● Shreveport

MISSISSIPPI

TEXAS

Mississippi River

● Alexandria

Mississippi River

Baton Rouge ★

Lake Pontchartrain

New Orleans ●

WELCOME TO THE 18th State!

GULF OF MEXICO

Bayou LaFourche

Name: _____

---

# CROSSWORD CLUES ··············

## ACROSS

**1.** The Big _____ is a nickname for the Mississippi River.

**3.** President Thomas _____ is responsible for the Louisiana Purchase.

**4.** The state of Louisiana is shaped like a big, fat _____.

**7.** Herons, _____, and other wildlife inhabit the bayous.

**8.** Because it's laid back, New Orleans is nicknamed the _____ Easy.

## DOWN

**1.** The _____ family from New Orleans is famous for jazz.

**2.** Earthen _____ protect New Orleans from sea and river water.

**4.** A _____ is a marsh with slowly moving water.

**5.** _____ means Tuesday and *Gras* means "fat."

**6.** _____ Rouge is the capital of Louisiana.

6

---

of—the Louisiana Purchase of 1803, when President Jefferson paid 15 million dollars to France to purchase land that doubled the size of our country. Southern Louisiana is Cajun country. Cajuns are descended from French Canadian settlers who were rounded up and set adrift in boats by the British. Some wound up in Louisiana, giving the state its special spice.

*Solve this riddle by placing the underlined letters in order on the blanks.*

# RIDDLE ··············

I am a bird with an enormous elastic throat pouch I use as a net to scoop up fish. I give Louisiana its nickname.

I am a _ _ _ _ _ _ _ .

3

# WELCOME TO LOUISIANA

Louisiana is shaped like a big, fat boot. The toe points to the Gulf of Mexico and Mississippi, the sole sits on the Gulf, and the boot top goes up to Arkansas. Although Louisianans don't need snow boots, they do need waders for the bayou country. The Big Muddy (the Mississippi River) flows through the state and fans out into bayous (marshes) full of alligators and herons before it empties into the Gulf. The state shares its name with—and was part

---

## LOUISIANA FAST FACTS ···········

**Population:** 4,468,976 (22nd largest)

**Size:** 43,562 square miles (31st largest)

**Year Admitted to the Union:** 1812 (18th state admitted)

**Average Temperatures:** January: 62 degrees; July: 90 degrees

**State Song:** "You Are My Sunshine"

**Famous Pirate:** Jean Lafitte

**Named After:** Louis XIV

**Louisiana First:** Tabasco sauce

> **The Marsalis family is the first family of jazz.**
>
> Ellis (piano), Branford (saxophone), and Wynton (trumpet) Marsalis are from New Orleans.

---

---

# NEW ORLEANS

New Orleans is located between the Mississippi River and Lake Pontchartrain. High levees have been built around the city to hold back the water. The city is nicknamed the Big Easy because it's laid back and tons of fun. Mardi Gras celebrations begin before the Tuesday preceding Lent (Fat Tuesday). The excitement consists of parades, floats, and outrageously beautiful costumes. The city is noted for music, especially jazz. Famed trumpet player Louis "Satchmo" Armstrong has a park named for him. The French Quarter boasts Spanish architecture and Creole cuisine (cooking).

Here are two more facts I found, or two thoughts I have, about the great state of MAINE:

1. _____

   _____

2. _____

   _____

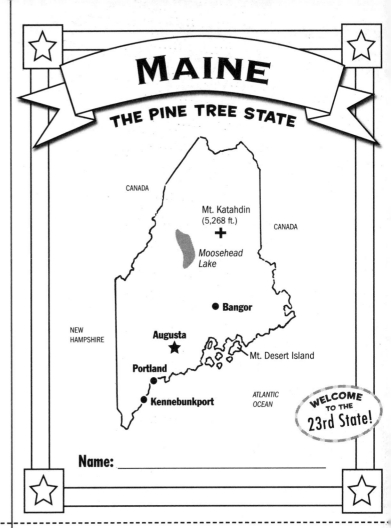

# MAINE
## THE PINE TREE STATE

CANADA

Mt. Katahdin
(5,268 ft.)

CANADA

Moosehead
Lake

● Bangor

NEW
HAMPSHIRE

Augusta ★

Mt. Desert Island

Portland ●

ATLANTIC
OCEAN

● Kennebunkport

WELCOME
TO THE
23rd State!

Name: _____

---

# CROSSWORD CLUES ··············

## ACROSS

**1.** You may see a _____ in Maine's woods.

**2.** _____ Mountain is on Mount Desert Island.

**5.** _____ Harbor is a popular tourist town.

**6.** The ocean water around Maine is very _____.

**8.** Mount _____ is in forever-wild Baxter State Park.

**9.** The capital of Maine is _____.

## DOWN

**1.** The only state farther north than _____ is Alaska.

**3.** The _____ Trail runs from Maine to Georgia.

**4.** If you like to eat _____, Maine is the place to go.

**7.** _____ National Park is on Mount Desert Island and Schoodic Peninsula.

---

lobsters thrive. Artists thrive there, too, rendering scenes of crashing waves, many-colored sunsets, and picturesque lobster boats. In 1775, the first sea skirmish of our Revolutionary War took place in Machiasport. After the battleship *Maine* exploded in Havana, Cuba, in 1898, "Remember the Maine" became the rallying cry of the Spanish American War.

*Solve this riddle by placing the underlined letters in order on the blanks.*

# RIDDLE ··············

Maine has over 60 of me. Traditionally, I serve as a beacon to ships at sea.

I am a _ _ _ _ _ _ _ _ _ _ .

# WELCOME TO MAINE

At 5,268 feet, Mount Katahdin rises majestically in Maine's Baxter Park, which is home to a variety of wildlife—moose included. The mountain is the beginning of the Appalachian Trail. Every year, thousands of hikers trudge over 2,000 miles from Springer Mountain in Georgia to Maine. The most northern of our 48 contiguous (touching) states, Maine has 3,000 miles of rocky, craggy coastline that is indented by bays and harbors—cold water where

2

## MAINE FAST FACTS

**Population:** 1,274,923 (40th largest)

**Size:** 30,862 square miles (39th largest)

**Year Admitted to the Union:** 1820 (23rd state admitted)

**Easternmost Point in U.S.:** West Quoddy Head

**First Woman to Serve in Both Houses of Congress:** Margaret Chase Smith

**State Bird:** Chickadee

**State Cat:** Maine coon cat

**Presidential Home:** The Bush home in Kennebunkport

---

**This once thriving Maine industry went bust.**

Ice is no longer cut and shipped for refrigeration.

4

7

# ACADIA NATIONAL PARK

Acadia, our first national park in the East, consists of a forested area on Mount Desert Island that is topped by Cadillac Mountain. Another rugged 2,000 acres sit on the mainland at Schoodic Peninsula. Carriage roads were built by John D. Rockefeller in 1913. Closed to cars, today these roads are thronged with cyclists and hikers. Tourists enjoying the sights on the Park Loop Road stop at the Jordan Pond House for popovers. Echo Lake offers swimming in warm, fresh water. Sand Beach has cold, sea bathing. Although it is not in the park, nearby Bar Harbor beckons many tourists with its shops and hotels.

5

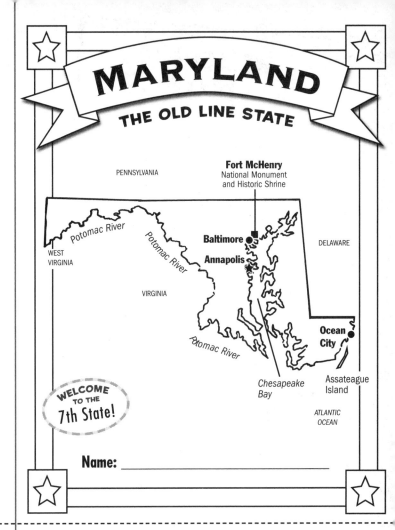

# MARYLAND
## THE OLD LINE STATE

PENNSYLVANIA

Fort McHenry
National Monument
and Historic Shrine

WEST
VIRGINIA

Potomac River

Potomac River

Baltimore

Annapolis

VIRGINIA

Potomac River

DELAWARE

Ocean
City

Chesapeake
Bay

Assateague
Island

ATLANTIC
OCEAN

WELCOME
TO THE
7th State!

Name: _____

---

**Here are two more facts I found, or two thoughts I have, about the great state of MARYLAND:**

1. _____
   _____

2. _____
   _____

Answer to Riddle: Harriet Tubman
Answers to Crossword: Across: 1. Chesapeake 3. Crabs 7. Baltimore 9. Declaration
10. Tubman; Down: 2. Spangled 4. Assateague 5. Seventh 6. Academy 8. Babe

(8)

---

# CROSSWORD CLUES ·············

## ACROSS

**1.** The _____ Bay opens to the Atlantic Ocean.

**3.** Maryland is famous for its delicious blue _____.

**7.** The city of _____ is named after Lord _____.

**9.** Four signers of the _____ of Independence lived in Annapolis.

**10.** Harriet _____ helped 300 slaves to freedom.

## DOWN

**2.** Our national anthem is the "Star- _____ Banner."

**4.** Chincoteague ponies live on _____ Island.

**5.** Maryland was the _____ state to join our Union.

**6.** The United States Naval _____ is at Annapolis.

**8.** The baseball player, George Herman Ruth, was called _____.

(6)

---

shelters <u>m</u>igrating peregrine falcons and Chincoteague ponies. The ponies are thought to be descended from horses that swam to safety from a wrecked Sp<u>a</u>nish galleon (ship) in the 1500s. Western Maryland has mountains and the Presi<u>d</u>ential retreat, *Camp David*.

## RIDDLE ·············

Solve this riddle by placing the underlined letters in order on the blanks.

Born into slavery in Cambridge, Maryland, in 1820, I escaped and helped 300 others to freedom by following the North Star.

I am _ _ _ _ _ _ _ _ _ _ _ _ .

(3)

# WELCOME TO MARYLAND

**M**aryland's blue crabs love the murky waters of the Chesapeake Bay. Four hundred miles of rivers feed into the bay, which opens to the Atlantic Ocean. It is the perfect location for the U.S. Naval Academy in Annapolis, one of our oldest cities. The city served as the nation's capital from 1783–84 and has four homes that belonged to Maryland's signers of the Declaration of Independence. Ocean City, a popular resort town, occupies a 10-mile barrier island, and nearby Assateague Island

## MARYLAND FAST FACTS

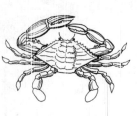

**Population:** 5,296,486 (19th largest)

**Size:** 9,774 square miles (42nd largest)

**Year Admitted to the Union:** 1788
(7th state admitted)

**Famous Poet:** Edgar Allan Poe (born in Boston in 1809)

**Famous Baseball Player:** George Herman "Babe" Ruth

**State Flower:** Black-eyed susan

**Famous Border:** Mason–Dixon Line (resolved border dispute with Pennsylvania)

**Big Industry:** Governmental Services (state is near Washington, D.C.)

> **Lord Baltimore gave his name to a major city.**
>
> The state bird—the Baltimore Oriole— carries his name, too.

# THE STAR-SPANGLED BANNER

**L**awyer Francis Scott Key sailed from Baltimore in 1814 to try to get his friend, Dr. William Beanes, released from British custody during the War of 1812. Key was then trapped on a ship throughout the 25-hour bombardment of Fort McHenry, which protected the mouth of Baltimore's harbor. As Key watched the bombing, he wrote the words to what is now our national anthem, the "Star-Spangled Banner." Fort McHenry was active in all our wars up to and including World War II. It still sits proudly over Baltimore's Inner Harbor. The 1814 flag that Key saw is now being restored.

**Here are two more facts I found, or two thoughts I have, about the great state of MASSACHUSETTS:**

1. _____

_____

2. _____

_____

Answer to Riddle: Dr. Seuss
Answers to Crossword: Across: 3. Seuss 4. Provincetown 8. Basketball 9. Fish
10. Cranberries; Down: 1. Boston 2. Nantucket 5. Crispus 6. Marathon 7. Dallas

---

# MASSACHUSETTS
## THE BAY STATE

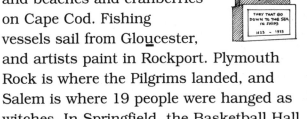

VERMONT

NEW HAMPSHIRE

NEW YORK

ATLANTIC OCEAN

Berkshire Hills

Concord

Boston

Massachusetts Bay

Springfield

Provincetown

Cape Cod

CONNECTICUT

RHODE ISLAND

Martha's Vineyard

Nantucket Island

ATLANTIC OCEAN

**WELCOME TO THE 6th State!**

Name: _____

---

# CROSSWORD CLUES ··············

## ACROSS

**3.** Dr. _____ was the pen name of Theodore Geisel.

**4.** _____ is on the north-eastern tip of Cape Cod.

**8.** Springfield is the home of the _____ Hall of Fame.

**9.** Folks sail in boats from the port of Gloucester to catch _____.

**10.** _____ are grown in the bogs of Cape Cod.

## DOWN

**1.** _____ is the capital of Massachusetts.

**2.** Martha's Vineyard and _____ are vacation spots off Cape Cod.

**5.** _____ Attucks was killed in the Boston Massacre.

**6.** The Boston _____ is our oldest annual long race.

**7.** President John Fitzgerald Kennedy was assassinated in _____, Texas.

---

Boston Harbor. Massachusetts has music and dance in the Berkshires and beaches and cranberries on Cape Cod. Fishing vessels sail from Gloucester, and artists paint in Rockport. Plymouth Rock is where the Pilgrims landed, and Salem is where 19 people were hanged as witch<u>e</u>s. In Springfield, the Basketball Hall of Fame tells a different kind of <u>s</u>tory.

*Solve this riddle by placing the underlined letters in order on the blanks.*

# RIDDLE ··············

I was born in Springfield and am the father of *The Cat in the Hat.* My name is Theodore Geisel, but

I'm called __ __  __ __ __ __ __ .

# WELCOME TO MASSACHUSETTS

Boston is chock full of history. The Old Granary Burial Ground holds the bones of John Hancock and Paul Revere. The city is the site of the Boston Massacre, where Crispus Attucks and four others were killed by British soldiers. Faneuil Hall, home to many furious political debates, is now a marketplace. At the Boston Tea Party, American patriots, some disguised as Indians, dumped 342 chests of tea into

---

---

# MASSACHUSETTS FAST FACTS ·······

**Population:** 6,349,097 (13th largest)

**Size:** 7,840 square miles (45th largest)

**Year Admitted to the Union:** 1788 (6th state admitted)

**Oldest Annual Long-Distance Race:** Boston Marathon (first run in 1897)

**First College in North America:** Harvard at Cambridge (established in 1636)

**State Fish:** Cod

**State Drink:** Cranberry juice

**First Thanksgiving:** Held at Plymouth in 1621

**Poet Longfellow called this "the shot heard 'round the world."**

The shot was fired in Concord, on April 19, 1775, beginning the Revolutionary War—our war for independence.

---

# PRESIDENT JOHN FITZGERALD KENNEDY (1917–1963)

In 1960, backed by a powerful and wealthy father and aided by a hard-working family, John F. Kennedy narrowly defeated Richard M. Nixon to become President. A hero of World War II, he had served in the Massachusetts House of Representatives and the Senate. He was not only the first Catholic President, but also the youngest President ever elected. Kennedy was much loved for his charm, speaking skills, engaging children, and beautiful wife, Jacqueline. In November of 1963, while riding in a motorcade in Dallas, Texas, he was shot and killed by Lee Harvey Oswald. His death caused an outpouring of grief throughout the nation.

Here are two more facts I found, or two thoughts I have, about the great state of MICHIGAN:

1. _____

_____

2. _____

_____

# MICHIGAN
## THE WOLVERINE STATE

Isle Royale National Park

LAKE SUPERIOR

Canada
U.S.A.

ONTARIO

**Sault Sainte Marie**

Mackinac Bridge

LAKE MICHIGAN

LAKE HURON

**Lansing** ★

**Detroit**

ONTARIO

**Battle Creek**

INDIANA    OHIO    LAKE ERIE

WELCOME TO THE 26th State!

Name: _____

---

# CROSSWORD CLUES ·············

## ACROSS

**5.** _____ Creek is the cereal capital of the world.

**6.** There are still some _____ in Michigan's Upper Peninsula.

**9.** Michigan is composed of two _____ joined by a bridge.

**10.** Berry _____, Jr., is the originator of the Motown sound.

## DOWN

**1.** Michigan's Lower Peninsula is shaped like a _____.

**2.** _____ is short for Motor City, which stands for Detroit.

**3.** The _____ Bridge is five miles long.

**4.** In 1903, _____ Ford and others founded the Ford Motor Company.

**7.** The capital of Michigan is _____.

**8.** The state of Michigan touches four of the five _____ Lakes.

accessible only by boat or float-plane. It has moose, beavers, loons, wolves, and a cold and blustery climate. The heavily populated and more temperate "mitten" is a manufacturing and agricultural powerhouse. The state is the birthplace of abolitionist Sojourner Truth, pilot Charles Lindbergh, and President Gerald R. Ford.

Solve this riddle by placing the underlined letters in order on the blanks.

# RIDDLE ·····················

I was designed by Henry Ford, came in one color (black), and was the first automobile that ordinary folks could afford.

I am a _ _ _ _ _ _ _.

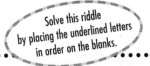

## WELCOME TO MICHIGAN

Michigan consists of two parts: the rugged Upper Peninsula and the mitten-shaped Lower Peninsula. The five-mile-long <u>M</u>ackinac Bridge connects them. The state touches four of our five Great Lakes: Superior, Huron, Michigan, and Erie, but n<u>o</u>t Ontario. The Soo Locks at Sault Sainte Marie bridge the 21-foot height <u>d</u>ifference between Lake Huron and Lake Superior to allow shipping between the lakes. Isle Royale National Park in the Upper Peninsula is

(2)

(7)

## MICHIGAN FAST FACTS ·············

**Population:** 9,938,444 (8th largest)
**Size:** 56,804 square miles (23rd largest)
**Year Admitted to the Union:** 1837 (26th state admitted)
**Cereal Bowl of America:** Battle Creek
**Historic Park:** Greenfield Village in Dearborn
**State Bird:** Robin
**State Reptile:** Painted turtle
**Inspiration for Car Names:** Chief Pontiac and Antoine Cadillac

**The state of Michigan has a long shoreline.**

It's longer than the coastline from Maine to Florida.

(4)

## MOTOWN

Motown is short for Motor City, which is a nickname for Detroit (the motor capital of the world). In 1903, Henry Ford and several partners founded the Ford Motor Company. The demand for the company's Model T was so strong that Ford designed an assembly line to make the manufacturing process quick and cheap. Cars moved along a conveyor belt, and each worker did one task over and over. The workers were well paid, and Detroit became a magnet for laborers. One auto worker, Berry Gordy, Jr., founded Motown Records and revolutionized popular music with a new sound.

(5)

Here are two more facts I found, or two thoughts I have, about the great state of MINNESOTA:

1. _____
   _____

2. _____
   _____

# MINNESOTA
## THE NORTH STAR STATE

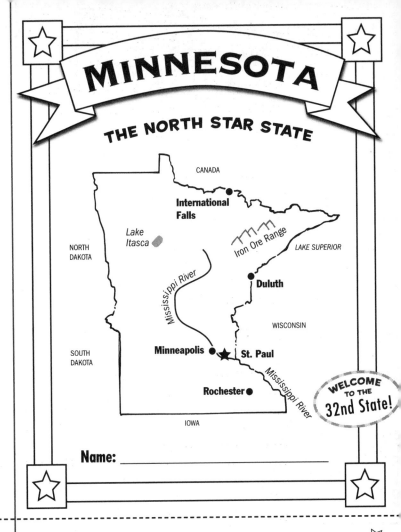

WELCOME TO THE 32nd State!

Name: _____

---

# CROSSWORD CLUES

## ACROSS

**2.** Hubert _____ and Walter Mondale were both Vice Presidents.

**5.** The Mall of _____ is our country's largest shopping complex.

**6.** The common _____ is the state bird of Minnesota.

**8.** Lake _____ is the largest fresh-water lake in the world.

**9.** The Minnesota _____ ball club is named for the Twin Cities.

## DOWN

**1.** Paul _____ is a legendary lumberjack who roamed Minnesota.

**3.** St. _____ is the capital of Minnesota.

**4.** _____ means "sky-tinted water."

**6.** _____ Ingalls Wilder was a famous author who lived in Minnesota.

**7.** _____ is a very important inland port on Lake Superior.

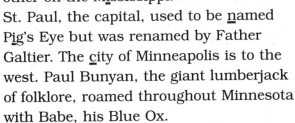

named after the "Twin Cities" of Minneapolis and St. Paul, which are directly across from each other on the Mississippi. St. Paul, the capital, used to be named Pig's Eye but was renamed by Father Galtier. The city of Minneapolis is to the west. Paul Bunyan, the giant lumberjack of folklore, roamed throughout Minnesota with Babe, his Blue Ox.

*Solve this riddle by placing the underlined letters in order on the blanks.*

# RIDDLE

I am world-famous for my medical expertise. Located in Rochester, Minnesota, I have treated over 4 million patients.

I am the _ _ _ _ _ _ _ _ _ .

# WELCOME TO MINNESOTA

I n the Dakota language, Minnesota means "sky-tinted water." The state has over 15,000 lakes and several powerful rivers, including the Mississippi. Lake Superior is the largest fresh-water lake in the world, and the major port of Duluth is situated on the lake. It is the western terminus (end) of the St. Lawrence Seaway. Iron ore and foodstuffs can be loaded on ships in Duluth and sent all the way to the Atlantic Ocean via the Great Lakes system. The Minnesota Twins baseball team is

2

7

## MINNESOTA FAST FACTS ·············

**Population:** 4,919,479 (21st largest)

**Size:** 79,610 square miles (12th largest)

**Year Admitted to the Union:** 1858 (32nd state admitted)

**Endangered Species:** Gray wolf

**Famous Vice Presidents:** Walter Mondale and Hubert Humphrey

**State Bird:** Common loon

**National Monument:** Pipestone (where only Native Americans may quarry clay for ceremonial pipes)

**State Flower:** Lady's slipper

> **Laura Ingalls Wilder wrote the *Little House* books.**
>
> **The series includes *Little House on the Prairie*, which inspired a TV series.**

4

# THE MALL OF AMERICA

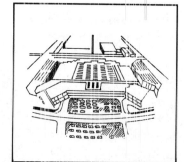

T he giant Mall of America is located in Bloomington, just outside the Twin Cities of Minneapolis and St. Paul. It is our country's largest retail and entertainment complex. Occupying 78 acres, the mall is a mix of stores, restaurants, and sights galore. A large indoor theme park tempts visitors with a roller coaster, log-flume, animal shows, and 3-D movies. LEGO has an imagination center in the mall. A two-level miniature golf course challenges players. A walk-through aquarium contains fish from Minnesota, the Mississippi River, and the Gulf of Mexico. It even has a coral reef!

5

Here are two more facts I found, or two thoughts I have, about the great state of MISSISSIPPI:

1. _____

_____

2. _____

_____

Answer to Riddle: Magnolia
Answers to Crossword: Across: 5. Faulkner 6. Eudora 9. Mississippi 10. Oprah;
Down: 1. Jackson 2. Magnolia 3. Delta 4. Presley 7. King 8. Civil

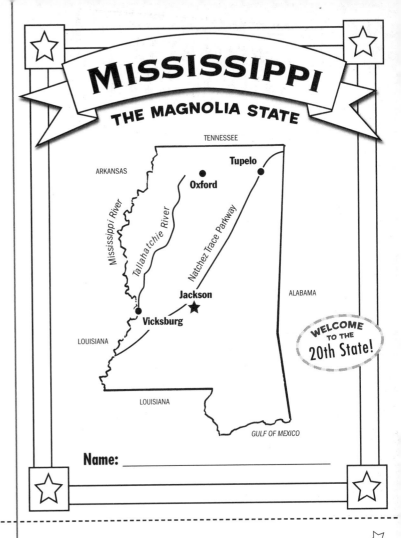

# MISSISSIPPI
## THE MAGNOLIA STATE

TENNESSEE

ARKANSAS

Tupelo

Oxford

Mississippi River

Tallahatchie River

Natchez Trace Parkway

ALABAMA

Jackson

Vicksburg

LOUISIANA

LOUISIANA

GULF OF MEXICO

WELCOME TO THE 20th State!

Name: _____

---

# CROSSWORD CLUES

## ACROSS

**5.** Many critics think William _____ is America's finest writer.

**6.** _____ Welty is another famous Mississippi writer.

**9.** The _____ River is strong, powerful, and changeable.

**10.** _____ Winfrey is a highly successful media star.

## DOWN

**1.** The capital of Mississippi is _____.

**2.** Mississippi is the _____ State.

**3.** Muddy Waters and B.B. King played the _____ Blues.

**4.** Elvis _____ was born in Tupelo.

**7.** Still a major crop, cotton was _____ in Mississippi at one time.

**8.** Our country's _____ War was especially hard on Mississippi.

---

won the Nobel Prize. Eudora Welty wrote into her nineties. Famed playwright Tennessee Williams and the authors John Grisham and Richard White all have roots in Mississippi. Ground-breaking music called the Delta Blues was perfected by Mississippians Bessie Smith, B. B. King, and Muddy Waters.

# RIDDLE

Solve this riddle by placing the underlined letters in order on the blanks.

I am a small tree or shrub and have gorgeous and colorful spring blossoms. I am the nickname for Mississippi.

I am a _____ _____.

# WELCOME TO MISSISSIPPI

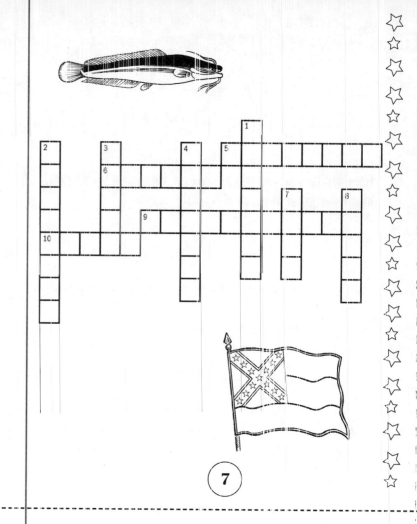

**T**he powerful Mississippi River dominates the state of Mississippi. The river floods and changes course, but it refuses to be tamed. Cotton is still an important crop in Mississippi, but once it was king. The Civil War caused severe destruction to the state and to its cotton economy. The South's defeat at the city of Vicksburg was a crucial blow to the Confederacy. Seventeen thousand soldiers from that battle are buried in the city. Some of our nation's finest authors are from Mississippi. William Faulkner (from Oxford)

---

# MISSISSIPPI FAST FACTS ............

**Population:** 2,844,658 (31st largest)

**Size:** 46,907 square miles (32nd largest)

**Year Admitted to the Union:** 1817 (20th state admitted)

**Ranked First in:** Catfish farming

**State Song:** "Go, Mississippi"

**State Bird:** Mockingbird

**Singing River:** Pascagoula

**Major Crop:** Cotton

**Elvis Presley was born in a "shot-gun" house in Tupelo.**

Elvis is the most successful solo recording star of all time.

---

# OPRAH WINFREY

**O**prah Winfrey is an amazing success story. An African American, she was born poor in Kosciusko Mississippi, and was mistreated as she grew up. Combining determination and hard work, she became a television reporter, anchor, and cohost of a morning show in Baltimore, Maryland. Then she was tapped for a show in Chicago, called *A.M. Chicago*. In 1986, the popular program was renamed the *Oprah Winfrey Show*, syndicated, and shown everywhere. Sensational at first, it became inspirational, and featured "Oprah's Book Club" to encourage reading. Oprah has acted in movies and has her own magazine.

Here are two more facts I found, or two thoughts I have, about the great state of MISSOURI:

1. _____

_____

2. _____

_____

Answer to Riddle: Harry S. Truman
Answers to Crossword: Across: 6. Truman 7. Kansas 8. Jefferson 9. Santa 10. Branson;
Down: 1. War 2. Disney 3. Music 4. Gateway 5. Hannibal

---

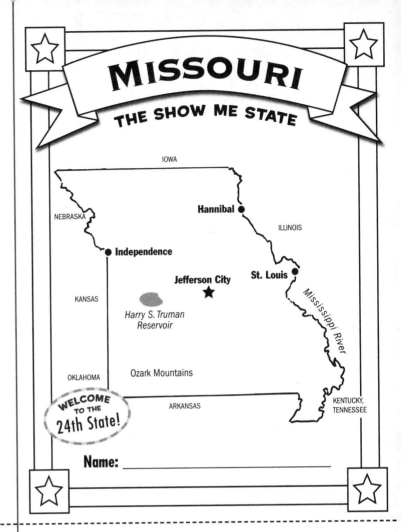

IOWA

NEBRASKA

Hannibal ●

ILLINOIS

● Independence

KANSAS

Jefferson City ★

St. Louis ●

Mississippi River

Harry S. Truman Reservoir

OKLAHOMA

Ozark Mountains

WELCOME TO THE 24th State!

ARKANSAS

KENTUCKY, TENNESSEE

Name: _____

---

# CROSSWORD CLUES ··············

## ACROSS

**6.** Harry S. _____ became President when Roosevelt died.

**7.** State Line Road divides _____ City, Missouri, from _____ City, Kansas.

**8.** The capital of Missouri is _____ City.

**9.** The California, Oregon, and _____ Fe Trails began in Missouri.

**10.** _____, the "Country Music Capital," has more shows than Broadway.

## DOWN

**1.** Winston Churchill led Britain during World _____ II.

**2.** Walt _____ spent his boyhood in Marceline, Missouri.

**3.** Missouri has a rich tradition in _____, including "Ragtime."

**4.** The _____ Arch in St. Louis celebrates Missouri's pioneer history.

**5.** _____ is the Mississippi River town where Mark Twain grew up.

---

rubble of a bombed-out London church. Kansas City, Kansas, and Kansas City, Missouri, are divided by State Line Road. The first U.S. shopping center, Country Club Plaza, and Crown Center (built by Joseph C. Hall of Hallmark Cards) enliven the city. Ragtime, jazz, and Branson's country music shows make Missouri a happenin' place.

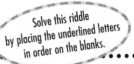

*Solve this riddle by placing the underlined letters in order on the blanks.*

# RIDDLE ··············

During World War II, I became President when FDR died in office. My motto was "The buck stops here."

I am ___ ___ ___ ___ ___ ___ ___ ___ ___ ___

# WELCOME TO MISSOURI

The Gateway Arch in St. Louis is the largest monument in the U.S. Since thousands of pioneers passed through the city on their way west, the city was considered the Gateway to the West. The Santa Fe, Oregon, and California Trails all began in Missouri. President Harry S. Truman's Presidential Library is located in Independence. In Fulton, tribute is paid to Britain's World War II leader, Winston Churchill, with a monument built from the

## MISSOURI FAST FACTS ·············

**Population:** 5,595,211 (17th largest)

**Size:** 68,886 square miles (19th largest)

**Year Admitted to the Union:** 1821 (24th state admitted)

**Birthplace of Ice Cream Cones:** St. Louis World's Fair (1904)

**Covered 2,000 Miles in 10 days:** Pony Express riders from St. Joseph to California

**State Bird:** Bluebird

**Famous Musician:** Scott Joplin developed Ragtime.

**Great Baseball Player:** Lawrence Peter "Yogi" Berra

> Marceline, Missouri, was Walt Disney's boyhood home.
> It was used for the model of Main Street, U.S.A., at Disneyland.

# MARK TWAIN (SAMUEL CLEMENS)

Samuel Langhorne Clemens was born in 1835 in the Mississippi river town of Hannibal, Missouri. He adopted the name Mark Twain in 1863. *Mark twain* means "two fathoms (12 feet)." It is the depth of water in which a riverboat can safely travel down a river. Twain was apprenticed to work for a printer at the age of 13 and to a steamboat pilot at 21. In 1865, he published his first story, "The Celebrated Jumping Frog of Calaveras County." A well-traveled man, Twain was a popular lecturer and humorist and wrote *Tom Sawyer* and *Huckleberry Finn*.

Here are two more facts I found, or two thoughts I have, about the great state of **MONTANA**:

1. _____

   _____

2. _____

   _____

Answer to Riddle: Bitterroot
Answers to Crossword: Across: 3. Icon 4. Chisholm 6. Cowboys 7. Glacier 8. Fluctuate
9. Copper; Down: 1. Rodeo 2. Smokejumpers 4. Custer 5. Sky

---

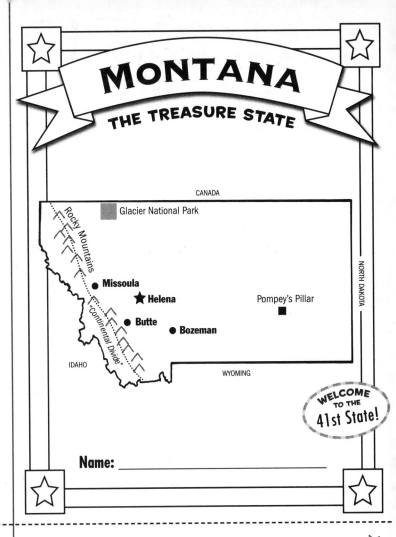

# MONTANA
## THE TREASURE STATE

CANADA

Glacier National Park

Rocky Mountains

NORTH DAKOTA

● Missoula

★ Helena

Pompey's Pillar ■

"Continental Divide"

● Butte

● Bozeman

IDAHO

WYOMING

WELCOME TO THE 41st State!

**Name:** _____

---

# CROSSWORD CLUES ·············

## ACROSS

**3.** An _____ is a symbol, as cowboys symbolize our West.

**4.** The _____ Trail ran from Texas to Kansas.

**6.** _____ are involved in the cattle business.

**7.** Driving-to-the-Sun Road is in _____ National Park.

**8.** To _____ means to go back and forth, or rise and fall.

**9.** At one time, _____ was mined in Butte, Montana.

## DOWN

**1.** Cowgirls and cowboys may participate in a _____ for prizes.

**2.** _____ are dropped from aircraft to fight forest fires.

**4.** General George _____ made his last stand at Little Bighorn.

**5.** Montana, which means "mountains" in Spanish, is Big _____ Country.

---

Divide) and into Glacier National Park. The pa_r_k is home to every type of mammal native to the U.S., 50 glaciers, and 100 lakes. The Little Big_h_orn National Monument c_o_mmemorates the battle between the Sioux and Cheyenne and U.S. forces led by General Custer. The U.S. Forest Service maintains a Smokejumper Base in Missoula.

*Solve this riddle by placing the underlined letters in order on the blanks.*

# RIDDLE ·····························

I am Montana's state flower, and a mountain range bears my name.

I am _ _ _ _ _ _ _ _ _ _ .

# WELCOME TO MONTANA

**G**old and silver were discovered in Montana in the 1860s. The Treasure State's huge copper deposits were mined for 100 years, making Butte the "richest hill on Earth." Today the treasure of Montana is the wide, open spaces of the Big Sky Country (another of its nicknames). Animals outnumber people in the state, and the temperature can fluctuate 100 degrees in one day! The Going-to-the-Sun Road takes visitors across Logan Pass (the Continental

MONTANA

## MONTANA FAST FACTS ...............

**Population:** 902,195 (44th largest)

**Size:** 145,552 square miles (4th largest)

**Year Admitted to the Union:** 1889 (41st state admitted)

**Movies Made in Montana:** The Horse Whisperer, A River Runs Through It

**State Motto:** Oro y Plata (means "Gold and Silver" in Spanish)

**State Animal:** Grizzly Bear (endangered in Montana)

**Roam Wild:** Wolves

**Nation's First Congresswoman:** Jeannette Rankin (a pacifist, who voted against our country's entry into both World Wars)

**Pompey's Pillar is named after Sacagawea's son.**

William Clark of the Lewis and Clark Expedition carved his name and the date into the pillar.

# COWBOYS

**C**owboys are icons (symbols) of the American West. Movies, advertising, music, TV, and art have popularized and romanticized their lifestyle. Expert ropers and horse handlers, cowboys branded and rounded up cattle from the open range. Then they drove the animals to market along miles of trails, such as the Chisholm Trail that ran from Texas to Kansas. The work was dangerous and dirty. Cowboys could encounter stampedes, dust storms, and floods. Today cowboys and cowgirls herd cattle on small and large ranches in Montana. They also participate in rodeos for prizes.

Here are two more facts I found, or two thoughts I have, about the great state of NEBRASKA:

1. _____

   _____

2. _____

   _____

---

# NEBRASKA

## THE CORNHUSKER STATE

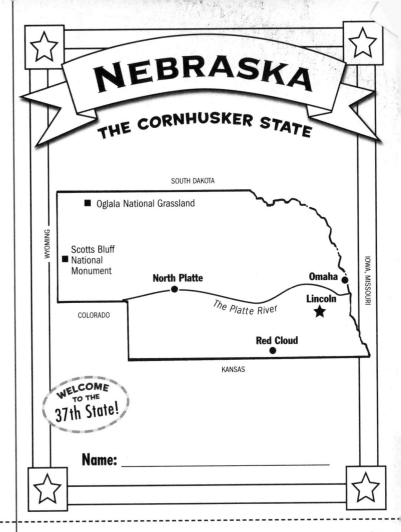

WELCOME TO THE 37th State!

Name: _____

---

# CROSSWORD CLUES ·············

## ACROSS

**3.** Chief Red _____ fought to have the Bozeman Trail closed.

**5.** J. Sterling Morton began _____ Day to encourage tree planting.

**7.** You can see the bones of a woolly _____ in a museum in Nebraska.

**8.** "He's not heavy, he's my _____" appears on a statue outside of Boys Town.

**9.** The _____ Act of 1862 encouraged settlers to move west.

**10.** The Bozeman, like the Oregon, California, and Mormon _____, guided pioneers.

## DOWN

**1.** Wagons, called *prairie* _____ "sailed" across the Great Plains.

**2.** The _____ River bisects (cuts in two) the state of Nebraska.

**4.** The Henry _____ Zoo in Omaha has a large indoor rain forest.

**6.** The _____ Trail carried prospectors to the Montana gold fields.

---

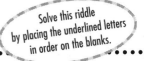

Homestead Act of 1862 promised 160 acres to any settler who farmed successfully for five years. Nebraskan J. Sterling Morton founded Arbor Day to encourage the planting of trees worldwide. Omaha's Henry Doorly Zoo sports the world's biggest indoor rain forest.

Solve this riddle by placing the underlined letters in order on the blanks.

# RIDDLE ·············

I am a proud member of the Corn Belt and love my nickname, which is the

_ _ _ _ _ _ _ _ _ _ _ State.

# WELCOME TO NEBRASKA

Woolly mammoths once roamed the Great Plains of Nebraska. At the University of Nebraska in Lincoln, bones of these giant beasts are on display. Buffalo replaced the mammoths, and now grasses and crops grow on the fertile plains. Pioneers on the Oregon, California, and Mormon Trails followed the course of the Platte River, which cuts across the middle of the state. The ruts from their iron-clad wagon wheels can still be seen. White-topped Conestoga wagons, or prairie schooners, looked like ships sailing across a sea of grass. The

## NEBRASKA FAST FACTS • • • • • • • • • • • •

**Population:** 1,711,263 (38th largest)
**Size:** 76,872 square miles (15th largest)
**Year Admitted to the Union:** 1867 (37th state admitted)
**Famous Author:** Willa Cather from Red Cloud
**Unique Government:** Unicameral (one-house) system
**Famous Leader:** Malcolm X
**Famous Actor:** Marlon Brando
**State Flower:** Goldenrod

> **You'll see the saying "He ain't heavy, he's my brother" in Nebraska.**
>
> It appears on a statue outside of Boys Town, near Omaha.

## CHIEF RED CLOUD (1822–1909)

Chief Red Cloud is said to be the only American Indian to defeat the U.S. government. As leader of the Oglala, Teton, and Dakota (Sioux), he was strongly opposed to the establishment of the Bozeman Trail because it crossed Indian lands protected by treaty. The trail, established by John Bozeman, drastically shortened the trip for prospectors traveling to the gold fields of the Montana Territory. Although the trail was protected by several forts, Bozeman and many soldiers were killed in Indian attacks along it. The trail was closed, and Red Cloud retired peaceably to a reservation.

**Here are two more facts I found, or two thoughts I have, about the great state of NEVADA:**

1. _____

_____

_____

2. _____

_____

_____

Answer to Riddle: Las Vegas
Answers to Crossword: Across: 5. Badwater 8. Census 9. Death 10. Silver;
Down: 1. Hoover 2. Highway 3. Bristlecone 4. Vegas 6. Tour 7. Carson

8

---

# NEVADA
## THE SILVER STATE

OREGON, IDAHO

CALIFORNIA

● Reno

★ Carson City

UTAH

Nuclear Test
Grounds (1950s) ■

CALIFORNIA

**Las Vegas** ●

*Lake Mead*

**Boulder City** ● Hoover Dam

*Colorado River*

ARIZONA

WELCOME
TO THE
36th State!

**Name:** _____

---

# CROSSWORD CLUES · · · · · · · · · · · · ·

## ACROSS

**5.** The lowest spot in the Western Hemisphere is near _____.

**8.** The U.S. _____ counts our population every 10 years.

**9.** In 1994, President Clinton made _____ Valley a national park.

**10.** Nevada's capitol building has a _____ dome.

## DOWN

**1.** The _____ Dam is on the border of Arizona and Nevada.

**2.** The Extraterrestrial _____ is really SR (State Road) 375.

**3.** _____ pines are the oldest living things on earth.

**4.** Las _____ has shows, sights, and excitement.

**6.** The _____ de France is a long-distance bicycle race.

**7.** The capital of Nevada is _____ City.

6

---

population has grown—a whopping 66.3 percent in 10 years! The Comstock Lode brought silver miners to Virginia City and furnished the silver dome for the capitol building. Route 50, the Loneliest Road in America, is an old Pony Express route with no services for miles. On the Extraterrestrial Highway (SR 375), "aliens" have been spotted!

**RIDDLE** · · · · · · · · · · · · · · · · · · · · · · ·

Solve this riddle by placing the underlined letters in order on the blanks.

I am the glittering show town that put Nevada on the map.

I am ___ ___ ___   ___ ___ ___ ___ ___ .

3

# WELCOME TO NEVADA

For five years 5,000 men worked around the clock in brutally hot and dangerous conditions to dam the Colorado River. Hoover Dam was completed in 1936. The dam provides flood control, water, and electricity. Water is stored behind the dam in <u>L</u>ake Mead, which is a recreation area. The dam made <u>a</u> difference in the life of the state by making the desert bloom. And the 2000 U.S. Census showed how much Nevada's

## NEVADA FAST FACTS ················

**Population:** 1,998,257 (35th largest)

**Size:** 109,826 square miles (7th largest)

**Year Admitted to the Union:** 1864 (36th state admitted)

**Famous Gangster:** "Bugsy" Siegel (started casino development in Las Vegas)

**Oldest Living Things on Earth:** Bristlecone Pines (can be 4,500 years old)

**Home of the Navy's "Top Gun" Flight School:** Fallon

**First Skier in U.S.:** John Thompson (skied to deliver mail in 1854)

**One of the Biggest Industries:** Tourism

**Greg LaMond, a cyclist from Nevada, was the first American to win the *Tour de France* (bicycle race).**

As a boy he rode 60 miles back and forth to school every day.

# DEATH VALLEY

Death Valley became a national park in 1994. Situated mostly in California, it straddles the Nevada border. It covers 3,336,000 acres and is a place of contrasts. Badwater, the lowest point in the Western Hemisphere, is 282 feet below sea level. Telescope Peak is 11,049 feet high! Temperatures have gone as high as 134 degrees F. Flash floods occur, but rainfall is less than two inches a year. American Indians have lived in the area for centuries, but Death Valley got its fearsome name in 1849 when some prospectors ran low on food and water. They never made it out of Death Valley.

**Here are two more facts I found, or two thoughts I have, about the great state of NEW HAMPSHIRE:**

1. _____

_____

2. _____

_____

Answer to Riddle: Mt. Washington
Answers to Crossword: Across: 4. Portsmouth 7. Velocity 8. Primary 9. Vermont
10. Smile; Down: 1. Granite 2. Challenger 3. Concord 5. Or 6. Notches

---

CANADA

Berlin

✛ Mt. Washington (6,288 ft.)

Old Man of the Mountains ■

VERMONT

MAINE

Lake Winnipesaukee

WELCOME TO THE 9th State!

Concord ★

Manchester ●

● Portsmouth

ATLANTIC OCEAN

MASSACHUSETTS

**Name:** _____

---

# CROSSWORD CLUES ··············

## ACROSS

**4.** _____ is New Hampshire's only seaport.

**7.** Mount Washington has the highest wind _____ (speed) ever recorded.

**8.** The earliest Presidential _____ was held in New Hampshire.

**9.** On a map, an upside-down New Hampshire looks like _____.

**10.** Winnipesaukee means the "_____ of the Great Spirit."

## DOWN

**1.** New Hampshire is the _____ State.

**2.** Teacher Christa McAuliffe was killed when the _____ exploded.

**3.** The capital of New Hampshire is _____.

**5.** The motto of New Hampshire is "Live Free ___ Die."

**6.** Retreating glaciers left _____ in the mountains of New Hampshire.

---

city at the end of an 18-mile beach. Over 300 islands dot Lake Winnipesaukee, which means "Smile of the Great Spirit." Other recreation spots beckon vacationers. General Stark, who fought with Washington during the Revolutionary War, is given credit for New Hampshire's stirring motto, "Live Free or Die."

*Solve this riddle by placing the underlined letters in order on the blanks.*

# RIDDLE ···························

I am the highest mountain in the northeast. My climate is like Antarctica, and I have the highest wind velocity ever recorded (231 miles per hour).

I am __ __.  ___ ___ ___ ___ ___ ___ ___ ___ ___ ___.

# WELCOME TO NEW HAMPSHIRE

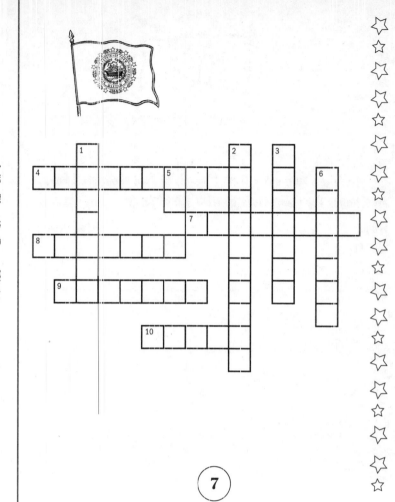

New Hampshire is called the Granite State because granite rock underlies most of it. Glaciers once covered the state with huge ice sheets. They retreated and cut notches in the mountains. They shaped the Old Man of the Mountains, a natural formation that looks like a face. Glaciers also left behind rocky soil, which is poor for farming. More of the state is forested today than it was in colonial days. New Hampshire has a port on the Atlantic Ocean. Appropriately named Portsmouth, it's an appealing

## NEW HAMPSHIRE FAST FACTS ·······

**Population:** 1,235,786 (41st largest)

**Size:** 9,024 square miles (44th largest)

**Year Admitted to the Union:** 1788 (9th state admitted)

**State Flower:** Purple lilac

**Covered Bridges:** Longest and oldest in the U.S.

**State Tree:** White birch (also called Canoe Birch)

**Upside-Down View:** Looks like Vermont

**Famous for:** Earliest Presidential primary

> **The first cog railway in the U.S. was built in 1869.**
>
> It still takes passengers up Mount Washington.

# CHRISTA McAULIFFE (1948-1986)

Christa McAuliffe, a married teacher with two children from Concord, was the first private citizen in space. President Reagan made the decision to give a teacher the opportunity to join the crew of a space shuttle. Over 11,000 teachers applied. Each state had two finalists. These were narrowed down to 10 and then to one—Christa McAuliffe. Her opportunity to participate in our nation's space program was tragically cut short when the *Challenger* exploded shortly after takeoff on January 28, 1986. Everyone on board was killed. A planetarium in Concord pays tribute to this dedicated teacher.

Here are two more facts I found, or two thoughts I have, about the great state of **NEW JERSEY**:

1. _____

_____

2. _____

_____

---

# NEW JERSEY
## THE GARDEN STATE

NEW YORK

Appalachian
Mountains

HUDSON RIVER

PENNSYLVANIA

● Newark

■ Sandy Hook
Lighthouse

★ Trenton

Delaware River

ATLANTIC OCEAN

DELAWARE

● Atlantic City

DELAWARE
BAY

Cape May ●

WELCOME
TO THE
**3rd State!**

**Name:** _____

---

# CROSSWORD CLUES ·············

## ACROSS

**5.** New Jersey is our most densely _____ state.

**6.** Manufacturing is big in the _____ State.

**7.** _____ is the capital of New Jersey.

**8.** The eastern part of New Jersey is on the _____ Ocean.

**9.** The symbol of the Republican Party is the _____.

## DOWN

**1.** The state flower of New Jersey is the _____.

**2.** The Wizard of Menlo Park was inventor Thomas _____.

**3.** George Washington crossed the _____ River on Christmas night.

**4.** The Jersey _____ is a 127-mile delight for vacationers.

**5.** Albert Einstein did research and taught at _____ University.

---

inventions in Menlo Park, and Albert Einstein developed his theories at Princeton University. New Jersey also has a firm place in our nation's history. On Christmas 1776, General George Washington crossed the ice-packed Delaware River and surprised and defeated the Hessians (German soldiers hired by the British) at Trenton.

*Solve this riddle by placing the underlined letters in order on the blanks.*

# RIDDLE ·····················

I carried water to the soldiers at the Battle of Monmouth in 1778. My husband was loading the cannon. When he was shot, I took his place.

I am _ _ _ _ _ _ _ _ _ _ _ _ .

# WELCOME TO NEW JERSEY

**A**lthough the Garden State is noted for its delectable tomatoes and other farm produce, manufacturing is the main staple of its economy. Our most densely populated state, New Jersey is conveniently located near some of our country's biggest cities. To the north is New York City, and to the west is Philadelphia. Washington and Baltimore are also nearby. Manufacturing is a powerhouse in the northern part of the state, but research takes place across the state. Thomas Edison worked on his

# NEW JERSEY FAST FACTS .........

**Population:** 8,414,350 *(9th largest)*

**Size:** 7,417 square miles *(46th largest)*

**Year Admitted to the Union:** 1787 *(3rd state admitted)*

**Legendary Creature of the Pine Barrens:** Jersey Devil

**First Dinosaur Skeleton Discovered in North America:** Hadrosaur *(at Haddonfield in 1858)*

**The Boss:** Bruce Springsteen *(born 1949 in Freehold)*

**Chairman of the Board:** Frank Sinatra *(born 1915 in Hoboken)*

**State Flower:** Violet

**The symbols of our major political parties were developed in Morristown.**
The elephant symbolizes the Republicans; the donkey represents the Democrats.

# THE NEW JERSEY SHORE

**N**ew Jersey boasts 127 miles of shoreline on the Atlantic Ocean. From the lighthouse at Sandy Hook to the ferry terminal at Cape May, the Jersey shore is open for visitors. To the north are Asbury Park and Ocean Grove. Bay Head, which is on a barrier island, offers views of Barnegat Bay and the Atlantic. Names like Beach Haven and Brigantine are familiar to vacationers. Atlantic City's street names are used on Monopoly boards. Ocean City and Sea Isle are quieter family resorts, while Cape May is known for its romantic Victorian atmosphere.

Here are two more facts I found, or two thoughts I have, about the great state of NEW MEXICO:

1. _____

_____

2. _____

_____

---

# NEW MEXICO

## THE LAND OF ENCHANTMENT

COLORADO

OKLAHOMA

■ Shiprock

● Taos

Los Alamos ●

★ Santa Fe

ARIZONA

● Albuquerque

Lincoln National Forest
(Home of Smokey Bear)

TEXAS

● Roswell

■
White Sands
National Monument

TEXAS

MEXICO

WELCOME
TO THE
47th State!

Name: _____

---

# CROSSWORD CLUES ··············

## ACROSS

**1.** The state bird of New Mexico is the _____.

**4.** _____ Fe is the capital of New Mexico.

**7.** The Navajo language was used to _____ messages during the war.

**9.** _____ Caverns is a magnificent collection of underground caves.

**10.** The first atomic bomb was detonated at the _____ Site.

## DOWN

**2.** The army said that the UFO found near _____ was a weather balloon.

**3.** New Mexico truly is the Land of _____.

**5.** _____ Indians make up the largest Indian group in the U.S.

**6.** _____ Bear helped prevent forest fires.

**8.** The _____ of six different nations flew over New Mexico.

---

Taos. Oil and natural gas, tourism, and research are important to the state's economy. The first atomic bomb was exploded at the Trinity Site in 1945. In 1947, the first reported crash of a UFO (unidentified flying object) was recorded near Roswell.

# RIDDLE ··············

Solve this riddle by placing the underlined letters in order on the blanks.

In 1950, I was a young bear cub clinging to a burned tree after a terrible forest fire. I became the symbol for the prevention of forest fires.

I am _ _ _ _ _ _ _ _ _ _ _ .

# WELCOME TO
# NEW MEXICO

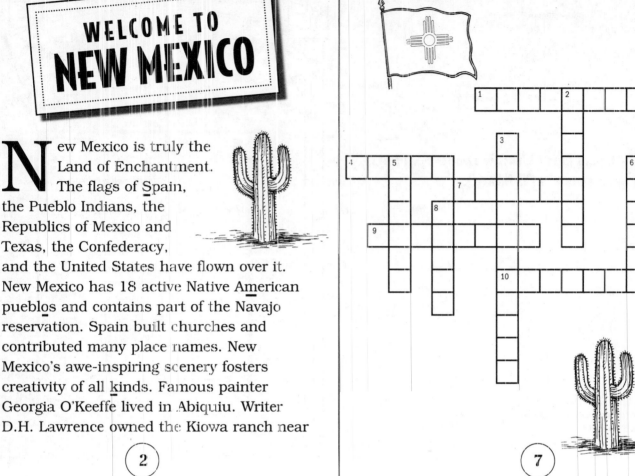

**N**ew Mexico is truly the Land of Enchantment. The flags of Spain, the Pueblo Indians, the Republics of Mexico and Texas, the Confederacy, and the United States have flown over it. New Mexico has 18 active Native American pueblos and contains part of the Navajo reservation. Spain built churches and contributed many place names. New Mexico's awe-inspiring scenery fosters creativity of all kinds. Famous painter Georgia O'Keeffe lived in Abiquiu. Writer D.H. Lawrence owned the Kiowa ranch near

2

7

# NEW MEXICO FAST FACTS ···········

**Population:** 1,819,046 (36th largest)

**Size:** 121,356 square miles (5th largest)

**Year Admitted to the Union:** 1912 (47th state admitted)

**Annual Festival in Albuquerque:** International Balloon Festival (hot air)

**Looks Like Snow:** Dunes at White Sands National Monument

**State Bird:** Roadrunner (It can run as fast as 15 mph.)

**Rock Formation Sacred to Navajo:** Shiprock

**Notable Crop:** Chiles (the most grown in U.S.)

**Carlsbad Caverns is the most magnificent cave system in the world.**
At dusk many thousands of bats emerge from the caves to feast on bugs.

4

# THE NAVAJO

**D**uring 1863–64, the U.S. government ordered Kit Carson to subdue the Navajo. He accomplished this by killing their herds and forcing 8,000 men, women, and children on a 300-mile walk (the Long Walk) across New Mexico to Fort Sumner. After four years in prison, the Navajo were released to reservation lands in New Mexico, Arizona, and Utah. Today there are over 200,000 Navajo. They are the largest Indian group in the U.S. The Navajo are famous for their rugs, painted pottery, and silver jewelry. Their complex language was used to encode messages during World War II.

5

**Here are two more facts I found, or two thoughts I have, about the great state of NEW YORK:**

1. _____

_____

2. _____

_____

Answer to Riddle: The Big Apple
Answers to Crossword: Across: 1. Island 3. Manhattan 5. Seneca 6. Terrorists 7. Erie
8. Finger 9. Niagara; Down: 2. Liberty 3. Million 4. Adirondack

---

# NEW YORK
## THE EMPIRE STATE

CANADA

Lake Placid

VERMONT

Lake Ontario

Adirondack Mountains

Lake Erie • Buffalo

Albany ★

Cooperstown •

CONNECTICUT

PENNSYLVANIA

WELCOME TO THE 11th State!

NEW JERSEY

Long Island

**Name:** _____

---

# CROSSWORD CLUES ··············

## ACROSS

**1.** Jones Beach is on Long _____.

**3.** _____ is one of New York City's five boroughs.

**5.** _____ Falls was the site of the first convention for women's rights.

**6.** _____ destroyed the Twin Towers of the World Trade Center.

**7.** The Great Lakes, _____ and Ontario, border New York State.

**8.** New York has 11 _____ Lakes

**9.** The mighty _____ River cascades over _____ Falls.

## DOWN

**2.** The Statue of _____ has welcomed millions of people to the U.S.

**3.** Over 7 _____ people live in New York City, our largest city.

**4.** The _____ Mountain Preserve has over 5 million acres.

---

play important roles in the state's economy. The <u>A</u>dirondack Mountain Preserve, which covers over 5 million acres and has 40 peaks higher than 4,000 feet, is the largest state or national <u>p</u>ark outside of <u>A</u>laska. Ringed by beaches such as Fire Island and Jones Beach, Long Island stretches into the Atlantic Ocean. In New York Harbor, the Statu<u>e</u> of Liberty raises her torch in welcome.

# RIDDLE ···········

*Solve this riddle by placing the underlined letters in order on the blanks.*

I am the nickname for the largest city in the United States (by population).

I am __ __ __   __ __ __   __ __ __ __ __ .

# WELCOME TO NEW YORK

The state of New York has something for everyone. Two Great Lakes, Erie and Ontario, grace its borders. The powerful Niagara River cascades over Niagara Falls. An awesome sight for tourists, the falls also supply hydroelectric power. Eleven scenic Finger Lakes are centered in New York's wine country. Agriculture is big in the Empire State, but education, research and development, manufacturing, and finance

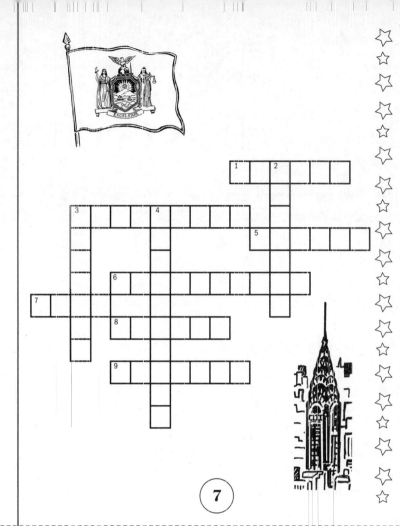

# NEW YORK FAST FACTS .............

**Population:** 18,976,457 (3rd largest)

**Size:** 47,214 square miles (30th largest)

**Year Admitted to the Union:** 1788
(11th state admitted)

**Baseball Hall of Fame:** Cooperstown

**Winter Olympic Games:** Held twice at Lake Placid (1932 and 1980)

**Most World Series Wins:** New York Yankees

**Immigration Museum:** Ellis Island in Upper New York Bay

**State Song:** "I Love New York"

**Suffragettes gathered in Seneca Falls in 1848 for the first women's rights convention.**

A national park celebrates women, like Susan B. Anthony, who were arrested for voting.

# NEW YORK CITY

New York City, the largest city (by population) in the United States, is made up of Manhattan, Brooklyn, the Bronx, Queens, and Staten Island. The city is home to over 7 million people, magnificent buildings, thriving businesses, and exciting sports teams. People can relax in Central Park or go to museums, Broadway shows, the United Nations, and Wall Street. Sadly, visitors to Manhattan can no longer take in the spectacular Twin Towers of the World Trade Center, which were destroyed by terrorists on September 11, 2001. The courage of New Yorkers since then has inspired the world.

**Here are two more facts I found, or two thoughts I have, about the great state of NORTH CAROLINA:**

1. _____
   _____

2. _____
   _____

Answer to Riddle: Blackbeard
Answers to Crossword: Across: 3. Textiles 5. Blackbeard 7. Raleigh 8. Outer
9. Hatteras; Down: 1. Shenandoah 2. Triangle 4. Devil 5. Blue 6. Dare

(8)

---

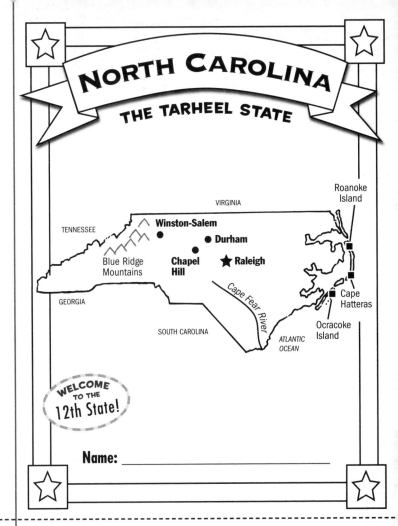

# NORTH CAROLINA
## THE TARHEEL STATE

VIRGINIA

Roanoke Island

TENNESSEE

Winston-Salem ●

● Durham

Blue Ridge Mountains

Chapel Hill

★ Raleigh

GEORGIA

Cape Fear River

Cape Hatteras

SOUTH CAROLINA

Ocracoke Island

ATLANTIC OCEAN

WELCOME TO THE 12th State!

Name: _____

---

# CROSSWORD CLUES ··············

## ACROSS

**3.** North Carolina leads in the production of _____.

**5.** The pirate _____ may have buried treasure on Ocracoke Island.

**7.** The capital of North Carolina is _____.

**8.** Erosion changes the _____ Banks every day.

**9.** The Cape _____ lighthouse was moved back 1,300 feet.

## DOWN

**1.** _____ National Park is in Virginia.

**2.** The Research _____ attracts students and job seekers.

**4.** The Wright Brothers flew their first airplane at Kill _____ Hills.

**5.** The _____ Ridge Parkway connects two national parks.

**6.** The first English child born here was Virginia _____.

(6)

---

North Carolina's fierce winds to propel their first airplane at Kill Devil Hills. Englishman John White started a colony on Roanoke Island, where his grandchild Virginia Da_re, the first European child born in the New World, was born in 1587. Returning from England with supplies, White found the colony deserted—and the wor_d Croatoan carved on a tree. The fate of the colonists is still a mystery.

# RIDDLE ··············

Solve this riddle by placing the underlined letters in order on the blanks.

I was a fearsome pirate who hid out on Ocracoke Island. Legend says I left behind buried treasure.

My name is _ _ _ _ _ _ _ _ _ _

(3)

# WELCOME TO NORTH CAROLINA

The Research Triangle of Duke University (Durham), North Carolina State University (Raleigh), and the University of North Carolina at Chapel Hill draws people seeking educations or jobs. The scenic Blue Ridge Parkway joins Shenandoah National Park in Virginia to the much-visited Great Smoky Mountains National Park. Biltmore, the 250-room Vanderbilt estate near Asheville, is America's largest private home. In 1903, Wilbur and Orville Wright took advantage of

---

---

# NORTH CAROLINA FAST FACTS ......

**Population:** 8,049,313 (11th largest)

**Size:** 48,711 square miles (28th largest)

**Year Admitted to the Union:** 1789 (12th state admitted)

**Leads the U.S. in:** Production of textiles

**State Bird:** Cardinal

**Famous Athlete:** Basketball player Michael Jordan

**Cherokee Town:** Many descendants of those who escaped the Trail of Tears, the forced march of the Cherokees to Oklahoma, live here.

**Venus flytrap eats insects and small animals.**
The plant is native only to small areas of North and South Carolina.

---

# THE OUTER BANKS

The Outer Banks consist of a 125-mile chain of islands and peninsulas along the North Carolina coast. Storms, wind, waves, and tides change these areas continually, and sometimes dramatically. Cape Hatteras National Seashore covers 45 square miles. At 208 feet tall, the black-and-white-striped Cape Hatteras lighthouse is the tallest brick structure of its kind. It was built to warn ships away from Diamond Shoals, the "Graveyard of the Atlantic." In 1999, in an amazing engineering feat, the lighthouse was moved inland 1,300 feet because severe erosion threatened its foundation.

Here are two more facts I found, or two thoughts I have, about the great state of NORTH DAKOTA:

1. _____

_____

2. _____

_____

---

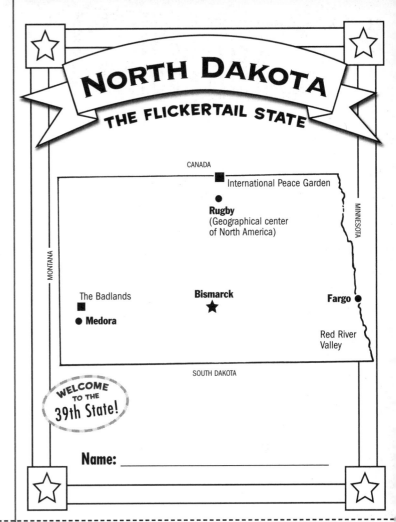

# NORTH DAKOTA
## THE FLICKERTAIL STATE

CANADA

International Peace Garden

Rugby
(Geographical center
of North America)

MONTANA

MINNESOTA

The Badlands

Bismarck

Fargo

● Medora

Red River
Valley

SOUTH DAKOTA

WELCOME
TO THE
39th State!

Name: _____

---

# CROSSWORD CLUES ··············

## ACROSS

**2.** American Bison are commonly called _____.

**4.** Theodore Roosevelt was _____ of the U.S. from 1901–1908.

**6.** North Dakota's capital, _____, is named for a German Chancellor.

**7.** Theodore Roosevelt was nicknamed _____.

**8.** The largest city in North Dakota is _____.

**9.** The U.S. shares the International Peace Garden with _____, Canada.

## DOWN

**1.** The _____ and Clark Expedition wintered in North Dakota.

**3.** The _____ State is nicknamed after a ground squirrel.

**4.** Most of North Dakota was obtained through the Louisiana _____.

**5.** Theodore Roosevelt's ranch was near _____.

---

Expedition wintered in North Dakota, which was largely acquired through the Louisiana Purchase. The northeastern part of the state was obtained from Great Britain in 1818. Every year 150,000 flowers are planted in the International Peace Garden, half of which is in Manitoba, Canada, to celebrate the friendship between the U.S. and Canada.

Solve this riddle by placing the underlined letters in order on the blanks.

# RIDDLE ··············

I am a rare albino (white) buffalo, sacred to American Indians. I live on protected land in Jamestown.

My name is _ _ _ _ _ _ _ _ _ _

# WELCOME TO NORTH DAKOTA

Fargo, North Dakota's largest city (population, 85,000), is named after William Fargo of Wells Fargo Express. Today most North Dakotans live in cities. Agriculture has become big business in North Dakota. There was a time when large herds of American Bison (popularly called buffalo) roamed the Great Plains, but they were almost killed off. Because the animals have adapted to North Dakota's harsh winters and their meat is lean, they are making a comeback. The Lewis and Clark

## NORTH DAKOTA FAST FACTS ·········

**Population:** 642,200 (47th largest)

**Size:** 70,665 square miles (17th largest)

**Year Admitted to the Union:** 1889
(39th state admitted)

**Geographical Center of North American:** Rugby

**Largest Statue of a Holstein Cow:** New Salem

**River That Flows North:** Red River

**State Bird:** Meadowlark

**Valley Celebrated in a Song:** The Red River Valley

**North Dakota
is the Flickertail State.**

A flickertail is a small ground squirrel
that flicks its tail in warning.

# THEODORE ROOSEVELT NATIONAL PARK

Theodore Roosevelt's wife and his mother died on the same day. Overcome with grief, Teddy retreated to a ranch in North Dakota in the badlands near Medora. He later said, "I would never have been President if it weren't for my experience in North Dakota." Once described as "hell with the fires put out," the badlands are eroded, windswept rock formations. Coal veins, set on fire by lightning, have burned the sand and clay into red scoria (a natural brick). Roosevelt's devotion to this landscape was honored with the establishment of the national park in 1947. It is the only U.S. national park named after a person.

Here are two more facts I found, or two thoughts I have, about the great state of OHIO:

1. _____

_____

2. _____

_____

Answer to Riddle: Son of Beast
Answers to Crossword: Across: 1. Buckeye 5. Columbus 6. Supreme 7. Armstrong
9. Buzzards; Down: 2. Ulysses 3. Cleveland 4. Glenn 8. Oberlin

---

# OHIO
## THE BUCKEYE STATE

MICHIGAN
LAKE ERIE
● Cleveland
PENNSYLVANIA
● Canton
INDIANA
★ Columbus
Son of Beast
Roller Coaster
Beach Waterpark
■
● Cincinnati
Hopewell Culture
National Historical Park
■
Ohio River
WEST VIRGINIA
KENTUCKY

WELCOME TO THE 17th State!

**Name:** _____

---

# CROSSWORD CLUES ··············

## ACROSS

**1.** Since its nut resembles the eye of a deer, the tree is called _____.

**5.** _____, the capital of Ohio, is in the center of the state.

**6.** President William Howard Taft also served on the _____ Court.

**7.** Neil _____ from Wapakoneta was the first person on the moon.

**9.** On March 15 _____ from the Smoky Mountains go to Hinckley.

## DOWN

**2.** Civil War general _____ S. Grant was our 18th President.

**3.** _____, on Lake Erie, is home to the Rock and Roll Hall of Fame.

**4.** At the age of 77, John _____ flew in the space shuttle *Discovery*.

**8.** _____ was the first college in the U.S. to accept both men and women.

---

Lake Erie, is home to the Rock and Roll Hall of Fame and the Great Lakes Science Center. Columbus is the capital. Cincinnati, on the Ohio River, has buildings connected by skywalks. Canton has the Pro Football Hall of Fame, and Chillicothe has the Adena State Memorial. In the Iroquois language, Ohio means "great." It sure is!

Solve this riddle by placing the underlined letters in order on the blanks.

# RIDDLE ··············

I live at King's Island and am the world's only looping wooden roller coaster.

I am the _ _ _  _ _  _ _ _ _ _ .

# OHIO

An industrial and transportation giant, the Buckeye State has produced several famous astronauts. In 1962, John Glenn was the first American to orbit Earth, and in 1998 he became the oldest person to ride into space on a space shuttle, the Discovery. On July 20, 1969, Neil Armstrong became the first person to walk on the moon. He said, "That's one small step for a man, one giant leap for mankind." Ohio has many important cities beginning with the letter *c*. Cleveland, on

## OHIO FAST FACTS

**Population:** 11,353,140 *(7th largest)*

**Size:** 40,948 square miles *(35th largest)*

**Year Admitted to the Union:** 1803 *(17th state admitted)*

**State Slogan:** "The Heart of It All!"

**Ancient Burial Mounds:** Hopewell Culture National Historical Park

**State Tree:** Buckeye

**First Co-Ed College to Enroll Men and Women:** Oberlin *(1837)*

**Female Astronaut:** Judith Resnik *(on board first flight of the shuttle Discovery)*

**Each year on March 15, buzzards descend on the town of Hinckley.**

**No one is exactly sure why this phenomenon occurs.**

# BIRTHPLACE OF PRESIDENTS

The state of Ohio has been the birthplace of seven Presidents. Ulysses S. Grant, our 18th President, is the general credited for winning the Civil War for the Union. Rutherford B. Hayes, the 19th to hold office, ended Reconstruction. James Garfield, the 20th President, was assassinated after only 150 days in office. Benjamin Harrison (23rd) is known for the Sherman Antitrust Act. William McKinley (25th) was also assassinated. William Howard Taft, our 27th President, later served as Chief Justice of the Supreme Court. Warren G. Harding (29th) became ill and died in office.

Here are two more facts I found, or two thoughts I have, about the great state of OKLAHOMA:

1. _____

   _____

2. _____

   _____

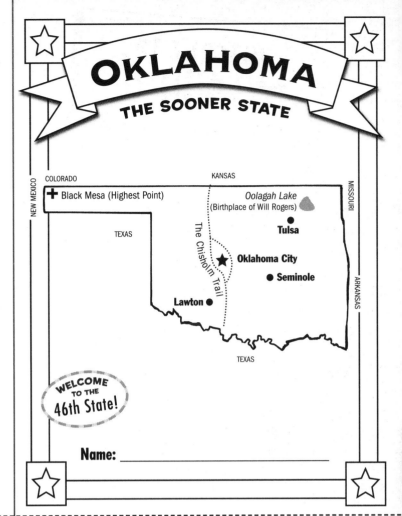

# OKLAHOMA
## THE SOONER STATE

COLORADO          KANSAS

NEW MEXICO

✚ Black Mesa (Highest Point)

*Oolagah Lake*
*(Birthplace of Will Rogers)*

TEXAS

The Chisholm Trail

● Tulsa

★ Oklahoma City

● Seminole

Lawton ●

MISSOURI

ARKANSAS

TEXAS

WELCOME TO THE 46th State!

Name: _____

---

# CROSSWORD CLUES ·············

## ACROSS

**4.** Oklahoma _____ is the capital of the state of Oklahoma.

**5.** Humorist Will _____ died in a plane crash.

**7.** Oklahoma used to be _____ Territory and Oklahoma Territory.

**8.** The National _____ Hall of Fame is in Oklahoma City.

**9.** Oklahoma is the _____ State.

**10.** The Oklahoma Land _____ began at noon on April 22, 1889.

## DOWN

**1.** John _____ wrote about the dust bowl in *The Grapes of Wrath*.

**2.** There are more _____ in Oklahoma than anywhere else.

**3.** The forced march of American Indians to Oklahoma was the Trail of _____.

**6.** Every county in Oklahoma has _____ wells.

of the capitol. A very windy place, Oklahoma is known as the tornado king. The dust bowl conditions of the 1930s created extreme hardship for farmers. Thirty-nine different Indian tribes live in the state. Many members are descendants of those who survived The Trail of Tears, a forced march from the southeastern United States.

Solve this riddle by placing the underlined letters in order on the blanks.

# RIDDLE ·············

I said, "I never met a man I didn't like." Born in Oolagah Indian Territory in 1879, I started performing rope tricks and became well known for my writing, humor, and philosophy.

My name is _ _ _ _   _ _ _ _ _ _ .

# WELCOME TO OKLAHOMA

**O**klahoma, a Broadway show and movie, has the stirring song "Oklahoma" as its centerpiece. The state celebrates its western heritage at Oklahoma City's National Cowboy Hall of Fame. Remnants of the Chisholm and other cattle trails crisscross the landscape. The nation's largest live-cattle auctions happen twice weekly at Stockyards City in the capital. Every county in Oklahoma has oil wells. Petunia #1 (a rig named after a discovery of oil in a flower bed) and other oil rigs adorn the grounds

(2)

---

(7)

---

## OKLAHOMA FAST FACTS

**Population:** 3,450,654 (27th largest)

**Size:** 68,667 square miles (18th largest)

**Year Admitted to the Union:** 1907 (46th state admitted)

**State Bird:** Scissor-tailed flycatcher

**Famous Folksinger:** Woody Guthrie

**State Flower:** Mistletoe

**Famous Country Singer:** Garth Brooks

**Famous Ballerina:** Maria Tallchief

> **"Get your kicks on Route 66."**
>
> Dubbed "Mother Road" by John Steinbeck, much of the road is still used today.

(4)

---

# THE SOONERS

**O**klahoma used to be divided into Indian Territory in the east and Oklahoma Territory (unassigned lands) in the west. Land "boomers" pressured the U.S. government to open up the west to homesteaders. At noon on April 22, 1889, prospective settlers lined up on the territorial border. Waiting for a pistol shot, they then made a rush to claim land. Those who occupied land before the legal start were called Sooners. More Oklahoma land was settled in a similar fashion, and cities of 10,000 grew overnight. The Indian and Oklahoma Territories joined to become the 46th state in 1907.

(5)

Here are two more facts I found, or two thoughts I have, about the great state of OREGON:

1. _____
   _____
   _____

2. _____
   _____
   _____

# OREGON
## THE BEAVER STATE

WASHINGTON

• Pendleton

Portland

✚ Mt. Hood (11,239 ft.)

Hells Canyon

PACIFIC OCEAN

★ Salem

IDAHO

• Eugene

◉ Crater Lake

CALIFORNIA    NEVADA

WELCOME TO THE 33rd State!

Name: _____

---

# CROSSWORD CLUES ··············

### ACROSS

**2.** _____ Lake was formed when the caldera of a volcano filled with water.

**3.** The capital of Oregon is _____.

**7.** The collapsed crater of a blown volcano is a _____.

**8.** The _____ Valley is very fertile and full of forests.

**9.** The state fish of Oregon is the _____ salmon.

**10.** Snow-capped Mount _____, near Portland, has several glaciers.

### DOWN

**1.** Mount Mazama was part of the _____ Mountain Range.

**4.** The Great _____ left Missouri in 1843.

**5.** _____, an inland port, is an important city in Oregon.

**6.** Blowing sand changes the Oregon _____ every day.

Roses has 200 parks. The Willamette Valley offers superb growing conditions and abundant forests. Many settlers came to Oregon looking for gold. In 1843, 1,000 pioneers, 120 wagons, and 5,000 head of livestock left Missouri to begin the Great Migration over the Oregon Trail. The gold's gone, but folks are still coming!

Solve this riddle by placing the underlined letters in order on the blanks.

# RIDDLE ··············

Sometimes people confuse me with a seal, but I have ears and live in caves in northern Oregon.

I am a _ _ _   _ _ _ _ _ .

# WELCOME TO OREGON

The people of Oregon are very conscious of the beauty of their state, and they work hard to protect it. Oregon has a 400-mile coastline on the Pacific Ocean, which is open to the public. The ever-shifting sand dunes of the Oregon Dunes National Recreation Area feature sightseeing, horseback riding, and exploring in off-road vehicles. The Willamette and Columbia Rivers meet and allow enough depth for an inland port at Portland. Sitting in the shadow of Mount Hood, this City of

# OREGON FAST FACTS

**Population:** 3,421,399 (28th largest)

**Size:** 95,997 square miles (10th largest)

**Year Admitted to the Union:** 1859 (33rd state admitted)

**State Fish:** Chinook salmon

**Leader in:** Production of plywood

**Two-Time Nobel Prize Winner:** Chemist Linus Pauling

**Named for Their Waterfalls:** Cascade Mountains

**City Named by the Toss of a Coin:** Portland

**There are different ideas about how Oregon got its name.**

These include *ouragan,* which means "hurricane," and *orejón,* which means "big-eared."

# CRATER LAKE

Over 7,000 years ago part of the Cascade Range erupted, blowing the top off of Mount Mazama. This eruption created a giant caldera, which is a crater caused by the collapse of a volcano's core. This particular caldera is six miles in diameter and 1,932 feet deep. Over the years, melting snow and falling rain have filled this crater with water and created the brilliantly blue Crater Lake. The lake has a 26-mile shoreline surrounded by lava peaks that are covered by snow for most of the year. Wizard Island, near the western shore, is accessible by boat. Crater Lake became a national park in 1902.

**Here are two more facts I found, or two thoughts I have, about the great state of PENNSYLVANIA:**

1. _____

_____

2. _____

_____

Answer to Riddle: Ben Franklin
Answers to Crossword: Across: 2. Lincoln 5. Keystone 6. Jefferson 7. Philadelphia
9. Hershey 10. Ben; Down: 1. Penn 3. Independence 4. Harrisburg 8. Amish

---

# PENNSYLVANIA
## THE KEYSTONE STATE

NEW YORK

Allegheny river

OHIO

Ohio river

**Pittsburgh**

Monongahela river

Allegheny Mountains

NEW JERSEY

★ **Lancaster**

**Harrisburg** **Philadelphia**

WEST VIRGINIA, MARYLAND & DELAWARE

Delaware Water Gap

WELCOME TO THE 2nd State!

**Name:** _____

---

# CROSSWORD CLUES ·············

### ACROSS

**2.** Abraham _____ dedicated the cemetery in Gettysburg in 1863.

**5.** Pennsylvania is the _____ State.

**6.** Thomas _____ wrote most of our Declaration of Independence.

**7.** Independence Hall and the Liberty Bell are in _____.

**9.** More chocolate is made in _____ than anywhere else.

**10.** _____ Franklin of Philadelphia was a man of many talents.

### DOWN

**1.** King Charles II granted William _____ land in what's now Pennsylvania.

**3.** The Declaration of _____ was signed and read on July 4, 1776.

**4.** The capital of Pennsylvania is _____.

**8.** Many _____ farm and lead simple lives near Lancaster.

---

prosperous. The state has always promoted religious tolerance. Its start goes back to 1681, when King Charles II of England gave a land grant to Quaker William Penn. During the Civil War, the Northern victory at the Battle of Gettysburg turned the tide for the Union. Abraham Lincoln's Gettysburg Address was given in November 1863 to dedicate the cemetery there. It's one of the greatest speeches of all time.

Solve this riddle by placing the underlined letters in order on the blanks.

# RIDDLE ·············

I was an inventor, writer, publisher, scientist, statesman, and philosopher from Philadelphia.

My name is _ _ _ _ _ _ _ _ _ _ _ _ .

# WELCOME TO PENNSYLVANIA

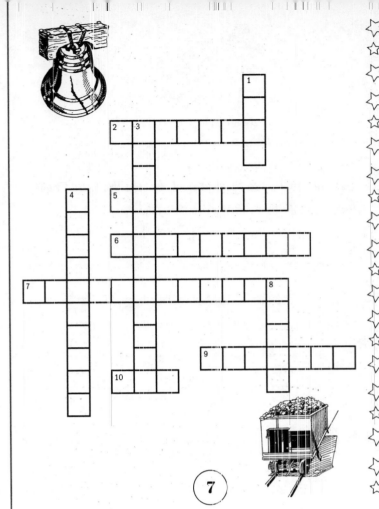

**A** keystone is the central stone that holds the two sides of an arch together. Pennsylvania, the Keystone State, was central to the creation of the United States. Philadelphia, the City of Brotherly Love, was home to the signing of the Declaration of Independence and the first and second Continental Congresses. Pennsylvania was the second state to ratify our Constitution. Steel, coal, agriculture, and manufacturing make it

2

7

## PENNSYLVANIA FAST FACTS ·········

**Population:** 12,281,054 (6th largest)

**Size:** 44,817 square miles (33rd largest)

**Year Admitted to the Union:** 1787 (2nd state admitted)

**Home of Little League:** Williamsport

**Home of Chocolate Kisses:** Hershey

**Home of Punxsutawney Phil:** Groundhog that predicts end of winter

**Famous Home:** Fallingwater (designed by Frank Lloyd Wright)

**First Oil Well in U.S.:** Titusville

> **The Amish settled in Pennsylvania in the 18th century.**
>
> They farm, wear simple clothing, drive buggies, and shun telephones, electricity, and modern technology.

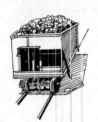

4

## INDEPENDENCE HALL

**B** uilt in 1732, Philadelphia's Independence Hall was the Pennsylvania state house. Frustrated with the heavy-handed rule of the British, several delegates to the Continental Congress called for independence in the hall. On July 4, 1776, "The Unanimous Declaration of the Thirteen United States of America" was approved. Mostly written by Thomas Jefferson, it was first signed by John Hancock. The Declaration of Independence was then taken outside the hall and read to a crowd of 8,000. After it was signed by the 56 delegates to the Continental Congress, the Liberty Bell rang out for freedom.

5

**Here are two more facts I found, or two thoughts I have, about the great state of RHODE ISLAND:**

1. _____

_____

2. _____

_____

Answer to Riddle: Block Island
Answers to Crossword: Across: 4. Amendments 6. Providence 7. Williams 8. Slater
9. Vote 10. Narragansett; Down: 1. Smallest 2. Newport 3. Rebellion 5. Stuart

---

# RHODE ISLAND
## THE OCEAN STATE

MASSACHUSETTS

MASSACHUSETTS

CONNECTICUT

Pawtucket ●

Providence ★

Narragansett Bay

WELCOME TO THE 13th State!

Jamestown ●   Newport ●

Newport Bridge
(links Newport to Jamestown)

Block Island

ATLANTIC OCEAN

**Name:** _____

---

# CROSSWORD CLUES ··············

## ACROSS

**4.** The first 10 _____ to the Constitution are called the Bill of Rights.

**6.** _____ is the capital of Rhode Island.

**7.** Roger _____ established what is now the state of Rhode Island.

**8.** Samuel _____ started our industrial revolution in Pawticut.

**9.** Universal suffrage is the right of everyone to _____.

**10.** _____ Bay is named after the _____ Indians.

## DOWN

**1.** Rhode Island, our 13th state, is our _____ state.

**2.** Very wealthy people built extravagant "cottages" in _____.

**3.** Dorr's _____ was about extending voting rights to more men.

**5.** Gilbert _____ painted a famous portrait of George Washington.

---

revolution. In 1842, Thomas Dorr led a rebellion to try to extend suffrage (the right to vote) to white men who did not own land. Convicted of treason, he was sentenced to a life in solitary confinement. Dorr was released after his ideas became popular.

# RIDDLE ··············

Solve this riddle by placing the underlined letters in order on the blanks.

I am a very popular family resort. You can only reach me by taking a ferry from Long Island, NY, Newport, RI, or Providence, RI.

I am _ _ _ _ _  _ _ _ _ _ _ .

# WELCOME TO RHODE ISLAND

The Massachusetts Bay Colony kicked Roger Williams out because he supported rights for American Indians and favored religious tolerance. In 1636, Williams founded "Rhode Island and Providence Plantations" on land he purchased from the Narragansett Indians. Rhode Island was the first colony to declare its independence from England. Our 13th and smallest state, Rhode Island is 48 miles long and 37 miles wide. Samuel Slater built a cotton-textile mill in Pawtucket in 1790, which began our industrial

# RHODE ISLAND FAST FACTS ·········

**Population:** 1,048,319 *(43rd largest)*

**Size:** 1,045 square miles *(50th largest)*

**Year Admitted to the Union:** 1790 *(13th state admitted)*

**Hall of Fame:** International Tennis Hall of Fame *(Newport)*

**Famous Artist:** Gilbert Stuart

**State Bird:** Rhode Island red

**State Motto:** Hope

**State Drink:** Coffee milk

**Newport is famous for its "cottages," the America's Cup yacht races, and the oldest U.S. synagogue (Touro).**
Built in 1895, Cornelius Vanderbilt's "cottage" is called the Breakers and has 70 rooms.

# THE BILL OF RIGHTS

Rhode Island refused to ratify the Constitution until the Bill of Rights was added. These first 10 constitutional amendments ensure individual rights and limit the powers of the federal and state governments. The first amendment guarantees the freedom of religion, speech, press, and the right to assemble peaceably. The second amendment allows citizens to bear arms. The fourth amendment forbids unreasonable search and seizures. The fifth amendment protects citizens from self-incrimination. A speedy trial (sixth), by a jury (seventh), without excessive bail (eighth), protects the accused. The 10th amendment reserves other powers for the people.

Here are two more facts I found, or two thoughts I have, about the great state of SOUTH CAROLINA:

1. _____

   _____

2. _____

   _____

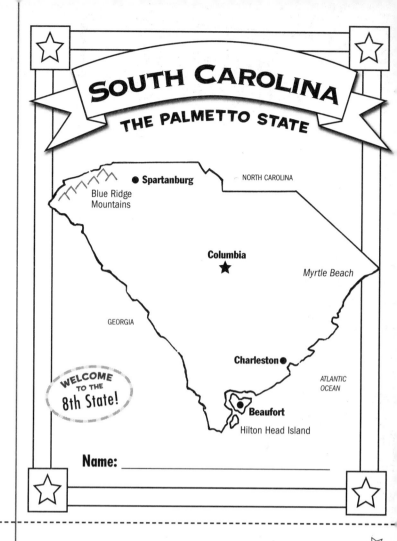

# SOUTH CAROLINA
## THE PALMETTO STATE

NORTH CAROLINA

Spartanburg

Blue Ridge Mountains

Columbia

Myrtle Beach

GEORGIA

Charleston

ATLANTIC OCEAN

WELCOME TO THE 8th State!

Beaufort

Hilton Head Island

Name: _____

# CROSSWORD CLUES ··············

## ACROSS

**1.** The _____ State has a _____ tree on its flag.

**4.** Eleven states joined the _____, which was headed by Jefferson Davis.

**5.** The gracious city of _____ overlooks the harbor.

**8.** The most battles of our Revolutionary _____ were fought in South Carolina.

**9.** The war between our North and South is called the _____ War.

**10.** South Carolina was the first state to _____ from the Union.

## DOWN

**2.** _____ Beach is a popular resort on the Grand Strand.

**3.** The capital of South Carolina is _____.

**6.** Hilton _____ Island is connected to the mainland by a bridge.

**7.** The first shots fired in our Civil War were at Fort _____.

during the Civil War have been restored. Enticing magnolia and cypress gardens are open to the public. Tourism is big in the state, and Hilton Head Island and Myrtle Beach on the Grand Strand are popular destinations. Agriculture, furniture making, and the manufacture of autos, textiles, and chemicals add more prosperity to the Palmetto State.

Solve this riddle by placing the underlined letters in order on the blanks.

# RIDDLE ··················

Legend says I am named after a pirate who terrorized the Atlantic coast. Today I am famous for crabs, clams, shrimp, and oysters.

I am __ __ __ __ __ __ __  __ __ __ __ __ .

# WELCOME TO SOUTH CAROLINA

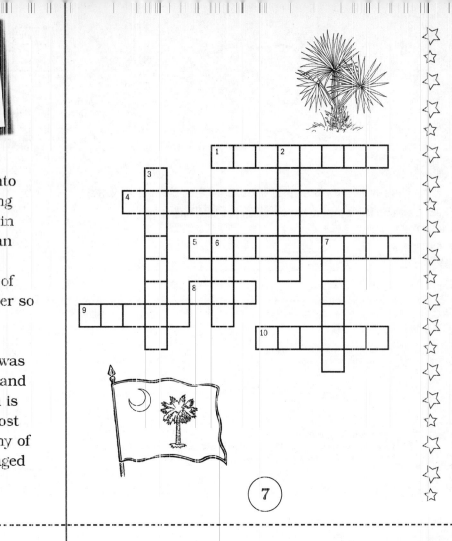

The Carolina Colony separated into North and South in 1729. During the Revolutionary War, soldiers in South Carolina fought more battles than anyone else—137 in all. On Sullivan's Island, patriots built Fort Moultrie out of palmetto trees. The logs were like rubber so the cannonballs bounced off, and the

British fleet in Charleston Harbor was defeated. Beautiful and historic, Charleston is South Carolina's most distinctive city. Many of the mansions damaged

---

# SOUTH CAROLINA FAST FACTS ·······

**Population:** 4,012,012 (26th largest)

**Size:** 30,110 square miles (40th largest)

**Year Admitted to the Union:** 1788 (8th state admitted)

**President Born in South Carolina:** Andrew Jackson

**State Fruit:** Peach

**State Flower:** Yellow jessamine

**Noted for Hammocks:** Pawleys Island

**Highest Point in State:** Sassafrass Mountain (3,560 feet)

> **After the Civil War, a group of former slaves remained on the Sea Islands.**
>
> Their distinct Gullah culture and language has retained much of its West African roots.

---

# FORT SUMTER

In 1860, South Carolina was the first state to secede from the Union over the issues of slavery, tariffs, and states' rights. Eventually, 10 other states joined the Confederacy. South Carolina demanded the return of all federal (U.S.) property within its borders—including Fort Sumter in Charleston Harbor. The fort refused to surrender. From April 12–14, 1861, South Carolina fired on it. The Civil War, one of the deadliest wars in history with 620,000 killed, had begun. After General Sherman's devastating march, which destroyed much of our South, the Union flag was again raised over Fort Sumter on April 14, 1865.

Here are two more facts I found, or two thoughts I have, about the great state of **SOUTH DAKOTA**:

1. _____

_____

2. _____

_____

Answer to Riddle: Corn Palace
Answers to Crossword: Across: 1. Wild 4. Rushmore 6. Badlands 8. Pierre 9. House;
Down: 1. Wounded 2. Fossils 3. Calamity 5. Wall 7. Crazy

---

# SOUTH DAKOTA
## THE MT. RUSHMORE STATE

NORTH DAKOTA

WYOMING, MONTANA

Crazy Horse Memorial

Pierre ★

● Rapid City

+ +

Custer ●

Badlands National Park

Mt. Rushmore

Missouri River

MINNESOTA, IOWA

● Mitchell

NEBRASKA

WELCOME TO THE 40th State!

Name: _____

---

# CROSSWORD CLUES ··············

## ACROSS

**1.** _____ Bill Hickok was shot dead holding a "dead man's hand."

**4.** Four great Presidents are depicted on Mount _____.

**6.** _____ National Park has an eerie but beautiful landscape.

**8.** The capital of South Dakota is _____.

**9.** Laura Ingalls Wilder is the author of the *Little* _____ book series.

## DOWN

**1.** The Sioux Indians fought twice at _____ Knee.

**2.** _____ of ancient mammals are buried beneath the Badlands.

**3.** _____ Jane could outshoot many men.

**5.** The _____ Drug Store in _____, South Dakota, advertises everywhere.

**7.** _____ Horse Monument will be the biggest statue in the world.

---

House books, lived for a time in DeSmet. Gold in the Black Hills brought settlers to the state. During two battles between the Sioux and the U.S. in 1890, 200 Native Americans were killed at a place called Wounded Knee. In 1973, 200 members of the American Indian Movement held it to protest the government's treatment of Indians.

# RIDDLE ··············

Solve this riddle by placing the underlined letters in order on the blanks.

I am decorated with murals made from colored corn and grains. Special events are held in me in Mitchell.

I am the ___ ___ ___ ___   ___ ___ ___ ___ ___ ___ .

# WELCOME TO SOUTH DAKOTA

Badlands National Park is in southwestern South Dakota. Underneath the ravines, ridges, and cliffs shaped by weather and erosion are the fossils of ancient mammals. Today, buffalo, bighorn sheep, eagles, and prairie dogs inhabit the eerie landscape. The nearby Prairie Homestead features a sod house complete with a piano. Serving tourists and locals is the Wall Drug Store, a combination museum, store, and restaurant that's advertised as far away as Australia. Laura Ingalls Wilder, author of the Little

## SOUTH DAKOTA FAST FACTS · · · · · · · · · ·

**Population:** 754,844 (46th largest)

**Size:** 75,885 square miles (16th largest)

**Year Admitted to the Union:** 1889 (40th state admitted)

**State Fossil:** Triceratops

**Great Shot:** Calamity Jane

**Famous Indian Chief:** Chief Sitting Bull

**Largest Gold Mine:** Homestake Mine in Lead

> **Wild Bill Hickok was shot dead while playing poker in Deadwood.**
>
> He was holding pairs of aces and eights, now called a "dead man's hand."

## MT. RUSHMORE AND CRAZY HORSE MEMORIAL

The Crazy Horse Memorial near Custer was commissioned by Lakota Chief Henry Standing Bear as a tribute to all North American Indians. When it is completed, the rendering of Chief Crazy Horse riding his pony will be the largest statue in the world (561 feet high and 641 feet long). In the Black Hills, the faces of four great presidents—George Washington, father of our country; Thomas Jefferson, author of our Declaration of Independence; Abraham Lincoln, savior of the Union, and Theodore Roosevelt, an early conservationist—are carved into Mount Rushmore.

**Here are two more facts I found, or two thoughts I have, about the great state of TENNESSEE:**

1. _____

   _____

2. _____

   _____

Answer to Riddle: Davy Crockett
Answers to Crossword: Across: 4. Hermitage 5. Authority 6. Mockingbird 8. Memphis 9. Elvis; Down: 1. Opry 2. Smoky 3. Nashville 5. Atomic 7. Davy

(8)

---

# TENNESSEE
## THE VOLUNTEER STATE

KENTUCKY, VIRGINIA

ARKANSAS, MISSOURI

Mississippi River

Nashville ★

Natchez Trace Parkway

Gatlinburg ●

Great Smoky Mountains

NORTH CAROLINA

● Memphis

Chattanooga ●

MISSISSIPPI, ALABAMA & GEORGIA

WELCOME TO THE 16th State!

**Name:** _____

---

# CROSSWORD CLUES ··············

## ACROSS

**4.** President Andrew Jackson's home is called the _____.

**5.** TVA stands for the Tennessee Valley _____.

**6.** The state bird of Tennessee is the _____.

**8.** Dr. Martin Luther King, Jr., was shot and killed in _____.

**9.** _____ Presley lived at Graceland in Memphis.

## DOWN

**1.** The Grand Ole _____ has never missed a broadcast since 1925.

**2.** The Great _____ Mountains are part of a national park.

**3.** _____ is the capital of Tennessee and the Country Music Capital.

**5.** The _____ bomb was developed at Oak Ridge.

**7.** _____ Crockett was killed at the Alamo in Texas.

(6)

---

War. After seceding from the Union in 1861, Tennessee soldiers fought at Chattanooga, Chickamauga, and Shiloh. The atomic bomb was developed at Oak Ridge, where research continues. The struggle for civil rights took place during the 1960s. Dr. Martin Luther King, Jr., was shot and killed in Memphis on April 4, 1968. He was there to support a strike of sanitation workers.

# RIDDLE ··············

Solve this riddle by placing the underlined letters in order on the blanks.

I was a frontiersman killed at the Alamo in Texas. In movies and on TV, I am portrayed wearing a coonskin hat.

I am _ _ _ _   _ _ _ _ _ _ _ _ .

(3)

# WELCOME TO TENNESSEE

Tennessee is flanked on the west by the Mississippi River and on the east by the Appalachian and Great Smoky Mountains. The TVA (Tennessee Valley Authority) was formed in 1933 during the Depression to improve economic conditions in the Tennessee River area in the center of the state. Dams provide flood control, transportation, and cheap electricity. The Volunteer State sent many soldiers to the War of 1812 and to the Mexican

---

# TENNESSEE FAST FACTS ............

**Population:** 5,689,283 (16th largest)

**Size:** 41,217 square miles (34th largest)

**Year Admitted to the Union:** 1796
(16th state admitted)

**State Bird:** Mockingbird

**Home of President Andrew Jackson:**
The Hermitage

**Created by an Earthquake:** Reelfoot Lake

**World War I Hero:** Alvin C. York

**Father of the Blues:** W. C. Handy

> **Elvis Presley, who lived at Graceland in Memphis, is called the King.**
>
> **He was the biggest solo recording star ever.**

# MUSIC CITY, U.S.A.

Nashville, the capital of Tennessee, is also the country music capital of the world. Over half of all single recordings come from its Music Row. George Dewey Hay started the Grand Ole Opry in 1925 as the "WLS National Barn Dance." This is the oldest continually-running radio show—it has never missed a broadcast. The Opry is now also a live stage show. It's housed in a giant entertainment complex called Opryland, which includes a huge hotel, television shows, and a paddle-wheel showboat called the *General Jackson*. Banking, insurance, and printing are big business in Nashville, too.

**Here are two more facts I found, or two thoughts I have, about the great state of TEXAS:**

1. _____

_____

2. _____

_____

Answer to Riddle: Stephen Austin
Answers to Crossword: Across: 1. Bush 2. Capital 4. Mexico 7. Houston 8. Lyndon
9. Lone; Down:1. Bluebonnet 3. Second 5. Cattle 6. Oil

(8)

---

# TEXAS
## THE LONE STAR STATE

OKLAHOMA

NEW MEXICO

ARKANSAS

LOUISIANA

Dallas

El Paso

Big Bend National Park

Austin ★

Houston

The Alamo

MEXICO

Rio Grande River

Gulf of Mexico

WELCOME TO THE 28th State!

Name: _____

---

# CROSSWORD CLUES

## ACROSS

**1.** The _____ family has had two Presidents of the United States.

**2.** Austin is the _____ of Texas.

**4.** Texas used to be a part of _____.

**7.** Sam _____ captured Santa Anna at San Jacinto.

**8.** Our 36th President, _____ Baines Johnson, was called LBJ.

**9.** Texas is called the _____ Star State.

## DOWN

**1.** The state flower of Texas is the Texas _____.

**3.** Texas is _____ only to California in population, and Alaska in size.

**5.** Our biggest producer of beef _____ is Texas.

**6.** _____ was discovered in Texas in 1901.

(6)

---

influences, as well as its Hispanic heritage. President George W. Bush, who was Governor of Texas, is the son of former President George H.W. Bush. This is only the second time a father and son have served as Presidents (the Adams family was the first). Another Texan, Lyndon Baines Johnson, became President in 1963.

# RIDDLE

Solve this riddle by placing the underlined letters in order on the blanks.

The capital of Texas is named after me, because I worked hard to secure our independence from Mexico.

I am __ __ __ __ __ __ __ __ __ __ __ __ __ .

(3)

# WELCOME TO TEXAS

A big and powerful state, Texas is second only to Alaska in size and to California in population. In 1901, oil was discovered in the state, and Texas is now our largest producer of petroleum products. The NASA Space Center in Houston, electronic and high-technology products, and agriculture are also important to the state's economy. Texas was a republic for 10 years, and Texans have an independent spirit. The state has been enriched by southern and western

(2)

(7)

---

## TEXAS FAST FACTS ·················

**Population:** 20,581,820 (2nd largest)

**Size:** 261,797 square miles (2nd largest)

**Year Admitted to the Union:** 1845
(28th state admitted)

**Animal With Armor:** Armadillo

**Leader in:** The raising of beef cattle

**Tops in:** Production of oil and natural gas

**State Dish:** Chili

**State Flower:** Texas bluebonnet

The name *Texas* comes from a Caddo Indian word and means "Hello, friend."

This Caddo word is also spelled *Texias, Tejas,* or *Teysas.*

(4)

## THE REPUBLIC OF TEXAS

Texas declared its independence from Mexico on March 2, 1836. Mexican President Antonio Lopez de Santa Anna sent troops to stop the rebellion. "Remember the Alamo!" became the rallying cry for Texas independence after all the defenders of the Alamo were killed. By staging a surprise attack, Commander Sam Houston won the Battle of San Jacinto and captured Santa Anna. Texas declared itself a republic, and the Lone Star flag flew over the capital of Austin for almost a decade. In 1845, Texas became the 28th state to join the United States.

(5)

Here are two more facts I found, or two thoughts I have, about the great state of UTAH:

1. _____

   _____

2. _____

   _____

Answer to Riddle: Golden Spike
Answers to Crossword: Across: 3. Dinosaur 5. Spike 6. Beehive 7. Government
8. Olympic; Down: 1. National 2. Brigham 4. Seagull 5. Salt 7. Glen

---

# UTAH
## THE BEEHIVE STATE

IDAHO

Great Salt Lake

WYOMING

Salt Lake City ★ ● Park City

● Provo

NEVADA

COLORADO

Zion National Park

Glen Canyon National Recreation Area

WELCOME TO THE 45th State!

● Hurricane

ARIZONA

**Name:** _____

---

# CROSSWORD CLUES ··············

## ACROSS

**3.** There are many _____ fossils in Utah.

**5.** A golden _____ joins the Union Pacific and Central Pacific Railroads.

**6.** Because Utah is industrious, it is nicknamed the _____ State.

**7.** Seventy percent of all land in Utah is owned by the U.S. _____.

**8.** The 2002 Winter _____ Games took place in Salt Lake City.

## DOWN

**1.** Utah has five _____ parks.

**2.** _____ Young led his followers to Utah and founded Salt Lake City.

**4.** The California _____ is the state bird of Utah.

**5.** The Great _____ Lake is four times saltier than the oceans.

**7.** Lake Powell is formed by the _____ Canyon Dam.

---

the giant Glen Canyon Dam on the Colorado River. Seeking religious tolerance, Mormons followed Brigham Young to Utah from Missouri. Numerous pioneers—many pulling handcarts—followed, and they have had a major influence on the state. Prosperous because of valuable mineral deposits, the industrious Beehive State is a very special place.

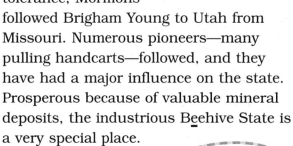

Solve this riddle by placing the underlined letters in order on the blanks.

# RIDDLE ··············

On Promontory Summit, Utah, I joined the Union Pacific and Central Pacific Railroad to form the first transcontinental railroad.

I am the _ _ _ _ _ _  _ _ _ _ _ .

# WELCOME TO UTAH

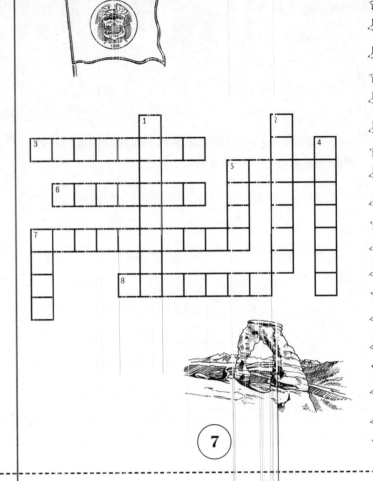

Named for the Ute Indians, Utah has some of our most spectacular scenery. These natural wonders are celebrated in five national parks, numerous state and local parks, and over a half-dozen national monuments. Over 70 percent of Utah is government-owned. The Great Salt Lake, salt flats, and deserts occupy the west. Canyons, reefs, and wind-sculpted arches and "hoodoos" dominate the south. The Lake Powell recreation area was created by

## UTAH FAST FACTS ·······················

**Population:** 2,233,169 (34th largest)
**Size:** 82,144 square miles (11th largest)
**Year Admitted to the Union:** 1896
(45th state admitted)
**Fossil Source:** Dinosaur National Monument
**State Bird:** California seagull
**Auto Speed Records:** Set at Bonneville Speedway on the salt flats
**First White Man in Utah:** James Bridger
**Highest Point:** Kings Peak (13,528 feet)

**In 1857-58, the Utah War occurred between Mormon authorities and the U.S. government.**

The issues were resolved, and in 1896, Utah joined the Union.

## SALT LAKE CITY

The very successful 2002 Winter Olympic Games were held in Salt Lake City. American athletes won more medals than ever before, and the games turned a profit. In 1847, Brigham Young founded the city with 148 of his followers. It is located at the south end of the Great Salt Lake, one of the saltiest bodies of water in the world. The capital of Utah is a commercial center and headquarters of the Church of Jesus Christ of Latter-day Saints (LDS or Mormon Church). The Mormon Temple and the Tabernacle, with its renowned choir, draw visitors from all over the world.

Here are two more facts I found, or two thoughts I have, about the great state of VERMONT:

1. _____

   _____

2. _____

   _____

---

# VERMONT
## THE GREEN MOUNTAIN STATE

CANADA

Lake Champlain

● Burlington

**Montpelier** ★

● Barre

**Middlebury** ●

NEW YORK

Green Mountains

Connecticut River

NEW HAMPSHIRE

● Bennington

WELCOME TO THE 14th State!

MASSACHUSETTS

**Name:** _____

---

# CROSSWORD CLUES ...............

## ACROSS

**2.** _____ produces more granite than any place in the world.

**5.** Noted for her folk art, Grandma _____ lived to be 101.

**6.** The Green Mountain Boys took Fort _____ from the British.

**7.** _____ means "green" in the French language.

**9.** _____ Allen was devoted to gaining statehood for Vermont.

**10.** American Indians called the maple sugar sap "_____ water."

## DOWN

**1.** Two _____ of the U.S. were born in Vermont.

**3.** The _____ horse was the only breed developed in the U.S.

**4.** _____ is the capital of Vermont.

**8.** Vermont is a big producer of cheese and other _____ products.

---

In French, vert means "green" and mont means "mountain." The Green Mountains run like a spine down the center of the state. Vacationers can enjoy beautiful scenery, hiking, and skiing. Lake Champlain offers all kinds of boating. The state is a big producer of marble. Barre has the largest granite quarries in the world.

# RIDDLE ..................

Solve this riddle by placing the underlined letters in order on the blanks.

The first exhibition of my paintings was in a drug store. Now my art is featured in a museum in Bennington, Vermont.

I am _ _ _ _ _ _ _ _  _ _ _ _ _ .

# WELCOME TO VERMONT

**V**ermont is our country's leading producer of pure maple syrup. Colonists learned the art of sugaring from American Indians. When the sap starts to run in late winter or early spring, taps are placed in the trees. Hanging buckets collect this "sweet water," which is transported by tubes to large kettles and boiled down. It takes 30 to 50 gallons of sap to make one gallon of delicious syrup for pancakes. Vermont also produces premium ice cream and fine dairy products.

## VERMONT FAST FACTS ·············

**Population:** 608,827 (49th largest)

**Size:** 9,250 square miles (43rd largest)

**Year Admitted to the Union:** 1791 (14th state admitted)

**Only Breed of Horse Developed in U.S.:** Morgan horse

**First State Constitution to Declare Slavery Illegal:** The 1777 Vermont Constitution

**State Tree:** Sugar maple

**First Postage Stamp Used in America:** Brattleboro area (in 1846)

**Presidents Born in Vermont:** Chester Arthur (21st), Calvin Coolidge (30th)

> **British author Rudyard Kipling wrote the *Jungle Book* and *Captains Courageous* in Vermont.** He lived in Brattleboro for four years.

# THE GREEN MOUNTAIN BOYS

**U**nder grants from New Hampshire, Ethan Allen and other settlers occupied land in what is now Vermont. Then the British decided the territory was part of New York. Allen, who was devoted to independence for his Vermont, gathered a fighting force together called the Green Mountain Boys. They managed to eject the Yorkers, as the intruders were called. During the Revolution, the Green Mountain Boys captured Fort Ticonderoga from the British and were successful at the Battle of Bennington. Allen worked hard to establish Vermont statehood. It became our 14th state two years after he died.

Here are two more facts I found, or two thoughts I have, about the great state of VIRGINIA:

1. _____

_____

2. _____

_____

# VIRGINIA
## THE OLD DOMINION STATE

MARYLAND; WASHINGTON, D.C.

Potomac River

Arlington

Chesapeake Bay

WEST VIRGINIA, KENTUCKY

Charlottesville

Richmond

Blue Ridge Mountains

ATLANTIC OCEAN

Virginia Beach

TENNESSEE, NORTH CAROLINA

WELCOME TO THE 10th State!

Name: _____

---

# CROSSWORD CLUES ..............

## ACROSS

**4.** The _____ has five sides.

**5.** Thomas Jefferson's home is called _____.

**7.** The _____ of the Unknowns has a guard 24 hours a day.

**9.** Skyline Drive runs in the _____ National Park.

## DOWN

**1.** The capital of Virginia is _____.

**2.** John F. Kennedy is buried at _____ National Cemetery.

**3.** Virginia Is for _____.

**4.** John Smith was saved by _____, daughter of an Indian chief.

**6.** General Robert E. _____ commanded the Confederate forces.

**8.** Virginia _____ is a popular seashore resort.

Navy's presence in Norfolk, the federal government is the state's largest employer. Virginia is full of historical places such as Colonial Williamsburg, Mount Vernon (Washington's home), Monticello (Jefferson's home), and the Appomattox Court House where Lee surrendered to Grant in 1865 to begin the end of the Civil War. Shenandoah National Park and Virginia Beach are beautiful vacation spots.

# RIDDLE ..............

Solve this riddle by placing the underlined letters in order on the blanks.

I am a large U.S. government office building with five sides. On September 11, 2001, terrorists attacked me, but I have been rebuilt.

I am the _ _ _ _ _ _ _ .

# WELCOME TO VIRGINIA

The first English settlement in America was founded in 1607 in Virginia at Jamestown. Virginia was the largest colony, and it contributed greatly to our fight for independence. Four of our first five Presidents hailed from the state. Richmond was the capital of the Confederacy, and many Civil War battles

took place in Virginia. As a result, poverty plagued the state until the two World Wars brought prosperity. With its proximity to Washington, D.C., many military camps, and the

## VIRGINIA FAST FACTS ··············

**Population:** 7,078,515 (12th largest)
**Size:** 39,594 square miles (36th largest)
**Year Admitted to the Union:** 1788 (10th state admitted)
**Most Presidents of the U.S.:** 8
**State Tree:** Dogwood
**Famous Native American:** Pocahontas
**Slogan:** Virginia Is for Lovers!
**Leader in Education:** Booker T. Washington

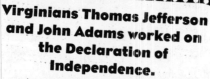

**Virginians Thomas Jefferson and John Adams worked on the Declaration of Independence.**

**Both men died on July 4, 1826 —the 50th anniversary of the Declaration.**

## ARLINGTON NATIONAL CEMETERY

General Robert E. Lee led the Confederate forces during the Civil War. In 1864, the U.S. government confiscated his estate, Arlington, which was across the Potomac River from Washington, D.C. Rows of white headstones mark the graves of U.S. veterans in what is now Arlington National Cemetery. Generals, government leaders, boxer Joe Louis, and World War II hero Audie Murphy are buried there. The grave of President John F. Kennedy has an eternal flame. Guards are on duty 24 hours a day at the Tomb of the Unknowns to honor soldiers whose remains have not been identified.

Here are two more facts I found, or two thoughts I have, about the great state of WASHINGTON:

1. _____
_____

2. _____
_____

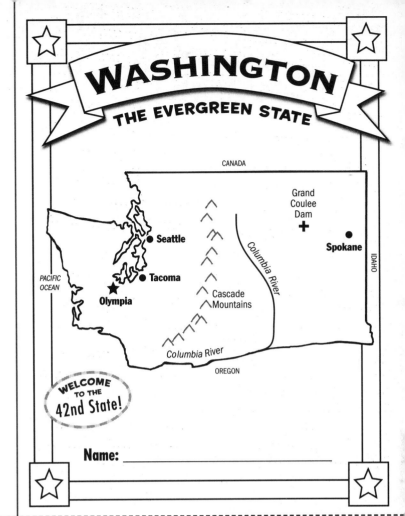

# WASHINGTON
## THE EVERGREEN STATE

WELCOME TO THE 42nd State!

Name: _____

---

# CROSSWORD CLUES ...............

## ACROSS

**2.** The Grand _____ Dam is one mile long.

**5.** _____ return from the ocean to fresh water to lay their eggs.

**6.** Seattle is on Elliott Bay in Puget _____.

**7.** Mount Rainier and Mount St. Helens are in the _____ Range.

**8.** Washington State is the world's champion at growing _____.

**9.** The Hoh is a rain _____ in Olympic National Park.

## DOWN

**1.** The capital of Washington is _____.

**3.** Visitors to Seattle enjoy the view from the Space _____.

**4.** Gold was discovered near the _____ River in the Canadian Yukon.

**5.** _____, an important city in the northwest, is named for an Indian chief.

---

Sound. Farther west, the Olympic Peninsula (with the state capital of Olympia) juts into the Pacific Ocean. A national park, Mount Olympus, the Hoh Rain Forest, (one of the few temperate rain forests in the world), and ancient trees enhance the state's unusual landscape. Spokane, Walla Walla, Yakima, and the Grand Coulee Dam are in the east.

Solve this riddle by placing the underlined letters in order on the blanks.

# RIDDLE ................

I am 605 feet tall and was built for the 1962 World's Fair in Seattle. Two revolving restaurants grace my top.

I am the _ _ _ _ _   _ _ _ _ _ _.

# WELCOME TO WASHINGTON

In 1896, gold was discovered near the Klondike River in Canada's Yukon territory. Thousands of prospectors moved into Seattle to prepare for that gold rush. Ever since then, folks seeking their fortunes have been coming to Washington, which is the home of Boeing and Microsoft. The Cascade Mountain Range divides the state into the rainy west and the arid east. Seattle, the dominant city in the Pacific Northwest, is located on Elliott Bay in Puget

---

---

# WASHINGTON FAST FACTS ··········

**Population:** 5,894,121 (15th largest)

**Size:** 66,544 square miles (20th largest)

**Year Admitted to the Union:** 1889 (42nd state admitted)

**Snowiest Town in the U.S.:** Stampede Pass (over 431 inches a year)

**World Leader in:** Apple growing

**Largest Totem Pole:** Tacoma (105 ft. tall)

**Only State Named After a President:** George Washington

**State Motto:** Alki (Indian word meaning "hope for the future")

> **Salmon are born in fresh water and swim to the ocean.**
>
> With great effort, they swim back to their birthplace to lay eggs (spawn).

---

# MOUNT ST. HELENS

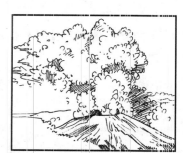

At 8:32 A.M. on May 18, 1980, the top and north face of snow-capped Mount St. Helens exploded. Smoke and hot ash shot 80,000 feet into the air. The shock flattened every tree for miles, and an avalanche of debris raised Spirit Lake at the base of Mount St. Helens by 200 feet. Logs clogged rivers, black night descended, and ash fell on cities hundreds of miles away. Other famous volcanic mountains in the Cascade Range, notably Mount Rainier, are currently dormant (sleeping). Mount St. Helens is now a national monument and attracts visitors with its incredible beauty.

**Here are two more facts I found, or two thoughts I have, about the great state of WEST VIRGINIA:**

1. _____
   _____
   _____

2. _____
   _____
   _____

---

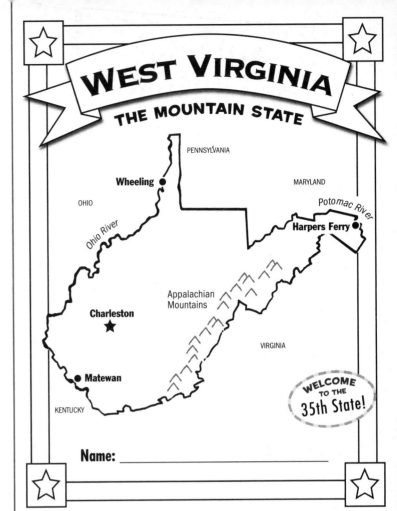

# WEST VIRGINIA
## THE MOUNTAIN STATE

PENNSYLVANIA

Wheeling ●

OHIO

MARYLAND

Potomac River

Harpers Ferry ●

Ohio River

Appalachian Mountains

Charleston ★

VIRGINIA

● Matewan

KENTUCKY

WELCOME TO THE 35th State!

**Name:** _____

---

# CROSSWORD CLUES ··············

## ACROSS

**1.** The mountain people of Appalachia excel in arts and _____.

**6.** The _____ Mountains begin in Canada.

**7.** The _____ and McCoys had the longest-running feud in U.S. history.

**8.** Attempts to unionize miners led to the _____ Massacre.

**9.** _____ mining is a big industry in West Virginia.

## DOWN

**1.** The capital of West Virginia is _____.

**2.** Because of opposition to _____, West Virginia became a separate state.

**3.** Incredibly strong, John _____ drove steel faster than a steam drill.

**4.** In 1863, West Virginia separated from _____.

**5.** _____-water rafting is a big sport in West Virginia.

---

contributed to the outbreak of the Civil War. The longest feud in U.S. history took place between the H̲atfields of W̲est Virginia and the McCoys of Ken̲tucky. Beginning with a murde̲r in 1882, the fighting continued until the 1920s. Coal mining and tourism, especially̲ white-water rafting, are big in the state.

*Solve this riddle by placing the underlined letters in order on the blanks.*

# RIDDLE ·······················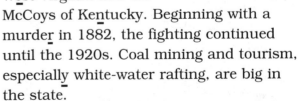

Legend says that I could dig a tunnel faster than a steam drill. I died with a hammer in my hand working on the Big Bend Tunnel in West Virginia.

I was _ _ _ _   _ _ _ _ _ .

# WELCOME TO WEST VIRGINIA

After our Revolutionary War, western Virginians began to oppose their state government. These mountain dwellers were against slavery, and in 1861, they voted against seceding from the Union. West Virginia became our 35th state in 1863. In 1859, abolitionist John Brown and a small band of followers captured the federal arsenal at Harpers Ferry. Robert E. Lee, then a colonel commanding U.S. forces, captured Brown two days later. Brown was tried for treason and hanged. The uproar that followed

# WEST VIRGINIA FAST FACTS ·······

**Population:** 1,808,344 (37th largest)

**Size:** 24,078 square miles (41st largest)

**Year Admitted to the Union:** 1863 (35th state admitted)

**State Motto:** Montani Semper Liberi (Mountaineers are Always Free)

**State Animal:** Black bear

**State Flower:** Rhododendron

**Soothing Waters:** White Sulphur and Berkeley Springs

**Showcase for Arts and Crafts:** Tamarack (opened in 1996 in Beckley)

**The Matewan Massacre occurred in 1920.**

Trouble broke out when the United Mine Workers tried to unionize the miners.

# THE APPALACHIAN MOUNTAINS

The magnificent Appalachian Mountains began with a geosyncline, or downbuckle, in the earth's crust. Originating in Canada, the Appalachians are some of the oldest mountains in the world. They include the White Mountains (NH), Green Mountains (VT), Catskills (NY), and Alleghenies (PA). Farther south are the Blue Ridge Mountains (VA, NC), Smokies (NC, TN), and the Cumberlands (TN). Mountain dwellers, especially West Virginians, are noted for their independent spirit. Celebrated for their quality music, art, quilting, and crafts of all kinds, the distinct mountain culture of the Appalachians adds beauty to the mosaic of America.

Here are two more facts I found, or two thoughts I have, about the great state of WISCONSIN:

1. _____

   _____

2. _____

   _____

Answer to Riddle: Harry Houdini
Answers to Crossword: Across: 3. Serpent 4. Cheese 6. Apostle 8. Houdini 9. GOP
10. Green; Down: 1. Superior 2. Democrats 5. Madison 7. Lincoln

---

# WISCONSIN
## THE BADGER STATE

Lake Superior

MICHIGAN

MINNESOTA

Green Bay

Wausau ●

Appleton ●

Oshkosh ●

LAKE MICHIGAN

● Ripon

IOWA

Mississippi River

Milwaukee ●

Madison ★

WELCOME TO THE 30th State!

ILLINOIS

Name: _____

---

# CROSSWORD CLUES ··············

## ACROSS

**3.** Winnebago Indians say the Dells were made by a giant _____.

**4.** Wisconsin, a major dairy state, is famous for _____.

**6.** Missionaries named the 22 _____ Islands, believing there were 12 islands.

**8.** Harry _____ from Appleton was a famous magician.

**9.** _____ stands for Grand Old Party, a nickname for the Republicans.

**10.** The Packers have made _____ Bay famous.

## DOWN

**1.** Two Great Lakes, Michigan and _____, border Wisconsin.

**2.** The _____ were named during the presidency of Andrew Jackson.

**5.** The capital of Wisconsin is _____.

**7.** Abraham _____ was the first Republican President.

---

dot the landscape. The Mississippi and Wisconsin Rivers add to the state's abundant water. The unusual Dells surround the Wisconsin River banks with fantastic forms cut into sandstone. The Winnebago Indians thought they were formed by a giant serpent. This scenery makes the state a tourist favorite. Noted for political activism, Wisconsin is the birthplace of the Progressive and Republican Parties.

Solve this riddle by placing the underlined letters in order on the blanks.

# RIDDLE ··············

I am a famous magician from Appleton, Wisconsin, noted for my daring escapes.

My name is _ _ _ _ _   _ _ _ _ _ _ _ .

# WELCOME TO WISCONSIN

**W**hen you think of cheese, think of Wisconsin. The state is our country's leading producer of dairy products. Or think of "cheeseheads"—the enthusiastic football fans of the Green Bay Packers. Green Bay lies on one side of the Door Peninsula, which extends into Lake Michigan. With Lake Superior on its northern border, Wisconsin dominates Great Lakes shipping. Over 15,000 smaller lakes

---

# WISCONSIN FAST FACTS ·············

**Population:** 5,363,675 (18th largest)

**Size:** 54,310 square miles (26th largest)

**Year Admitted to the Union:** 1848 (30th state admitted)

**Counted Incorrectly:** 22 Apostle Islands (originally counted as 12)

**Nation's First Kindergarten:** Watertown (1856)

**Circus Museum:** Baraboo

**Biggest Cheese:** 345,910 pounds (heavier than 3 elephants)

**First House in U.S. Wired for Electricity:** Appleton

> **Badgers live in caves dug in hillsides.**
> Early miners in the Badger State also lived in caves.

---

# THE REPUBLICAN PARTY

**T**he Grand Old Party (GOP) is the nickname for the Republican Party, which began in 1845 in Ripon. The party put national interests above local concerns. Opposition to slavery was its major platform. Abraham Lincoln, the first successful Republican candidate, won the presidency in 1860. Dominating elections for many years, the Republican Party has seen Theodore Roosevelt, Dwight Eisenhower, Ronald Reagan, and two Bush Presidents, father and son, elected as Presidents. The other major party, the Democrats, was formed in the 1830s during the term of Andrew Jackson.

Here are two more facts I found, or two thoughts I have, about the great state of WYOMING:

1. _____

_____

2. _____

_____

Answer to Riddle: Devils Tower
Answers to Crossword: Across: 1. Cheyenne 5. Devils 7. Cattle 8. Population 9. Tetons
10. Colter; Down: 2. Yellowstone 3. Equality 4. Wolves 6. Fumarole

# WYOMING
## THE EQUALITY STATE

MONTANA

Yellowstone National Park

● Cody    Bighorn Mountains    + Devils Tower

● Jackson

UTAH, IDAHO

SOUTH DAKOTA, NEBRASKA

● Laramie
Cheyenne
★

WELCOME TO THE 44th State!

COLORADO

Name: _____

---

# CROSSWORD CLUES ·············

## ACROSS

**1.** _____, the capital of Wyoming, is famous for Frontier Days.

**5.** _____ Tower is sacred to American Indians.

**7.** There are more _____ than people in Wyoming.

**8.** Wyoming has the smallest _____ of all our states.

**9.** The Grand _____ are mountains in northwest Wyoming.

**10.** John _____ was the first white man in the Yellowstone area.

## DOWN

**2.** The oldest national park in the world is _____.

**3.** The _____ State gave women the vote in 1869.

**4.** In 1995, gray _____ were introduced to Yellowstone National Park.

**6.** A hole in a volcanic area allowing hot gas to escape is a _____.

---

northwest corner. To the south is Flaming Gorge Recreation Area. Mining and tourism are beginning to rival raising livestock as major industries. The Equality State is noted for being the first place in the world to allow women the vote (1869). In 1925, Nellie Tayloe Ross was elected as the first female governor of any state.

Solve this riddle by placing the underlined letters in order on the blanks.

# RIDDLE ·············

I am the core of an ancient volcano sacred to American Indians. In 1906, I became the first national monument.

I am _ _ _ _ _ _ _ _ _ _ _ .

# WELCOME TO WYOMING

**W**yoming has the smallest population of any U.S. state. There are about five people per square mile—fewer people than cattle! To pay tribute to its frontier and western heritage, the capital, Cheyenne, celebrates Frontier Days. The last full week in July is devoted to rodeos, chuck wagon feasts, wild-horse races, and parades. Mountains are plentiful in Wyoming, and the Continental Divide cuts across the state diagonally. The Grand Teton and Yellowstone National Parks occupy the

---

# WYOMING FAST FACTS

**Population:** 493,782 (50th largest)

**Size:** 97,100 square miles (9th largest)

**Year Admitted to the Union:** 1890 (44th state admitted)

**Largest in the Nation:** Coal reserves

**Name:** Delaware Indian word meaning "alternating mountains and valleys"

**Monument Featured in Movie:** Devils Tower in *Close Encounters of the Third Kind*

**State Flower:** Indian paintbrush

**State Motto:** Equal Rights

> **Buffalo used newly installed telephone poles as scratching posts.** Sometimes 30 or more lined up to take their turns.

---

# YELLOWSTONE NATIONAL PARK

**T**he Lewis and Clark Expedition sent John Colter to make contact with the Indians in what is now Yellowstone National Park. He came back with tales of geysers, boiling mud, fumaroles (a hole in a volcanic area), and hot springs. People assumed he was telling tall tales, made fun of him, and called the region Colter's Hell. Yellowstone, with its famed Old Faithful Geyser, became the world's first national park in 1872. Besides the spectacular scenery, the park is a refuge for elk, buffalo, bears, deer, bighorn sheep, antelopes, and gray wolves (since 1995). In 1988, massive fires destroyed one million acres of the park.